BARRY HINES was born in 1939 in the mining village of Hoyland Common near Barnsley, where his father was a miner. Barry played football for the England Grammar School team and, after leaving school, for a short time for Barnsley whilst working there as an apprentice mining surveyor. He studied Physical Education at Loughborough Training College and taught for two years in a London comprehensive school, before returning to the North.

His most celebrated book, *A Kestrel for a Knave*, was published in 1968, and the film version, *Kes* (for which he wrote the screenplay with director Ken Loach) won rave reviews and many awards. The book is now a set text for GCSE exams and has been widely translated.

Barry Hines' other work includes radio, TV and stage plays, such as *Billy's Last Stand* (Royal Court, 1970, BBC-TV 1971), *Speech Day* (BBC-TV Play for Today 1972), *The Price of Coal* (BBC-TV 1977; Nottingham Playhouse 1984), *Looks and Smiles* (ITV 1982, also directed by Ken Loach, produced by Tony Garnett; Best Contemporary Screenplay Award, Cannes Film Festival), *Threads* (BBC-TV 1984; Broadcasting Press Guild Best Single Drama Award), *Shooting Stars* (Film on Four, 1990), and *Born Kicking* (BBC-TV 1992, produced by Tony Garnett). He has written six other novels, including *The Gamekeeper*, filmed by Ken Loach for ATV (1980). He lives in Sheffield.

LAWRENCE TILL is Artistic Director of the Palace Theatre, Watford. Before that he ran the Octagon Theatre, Bolton, for eight years, directing over thirty productions. Earlier still he was at Contact Theatre, Manchester, and was Education Director at the Crucible Theatre in Sheffield. He has three times been nominated as Best Director in the Theatrical Management Association British Regional Theatre Awards.

Kes

adapted from
BARRY HINES'
A Kestrel for a Knave

by

LAWRENCE TILL

NICK HERN BOOKS
London
www.nickhernbooks.co.uk

A Nick Hern Book

This adaptation of *Kes* first published in Great Britain in 2000
as a paperback original by Nick Hern Books Ltd, 14 Larden Road,
London W3 7ST

Kes © 2000 Barry Hines and Lawrence Till

Lawrence Till and Barry Hines have asserted their rights to be
identified as the authors of this work

Cover from photo copyright RSPB images, used with permission

Typeset by County Setting, Kingsdown, Kent CT14 8ES
Printed and bound in Great Britain by Biddles Ltd
King's Lynn, Norfolk

ISBN 1 85459 486 9

A CIP catalogue record for this book is available from
the British Library

Introduction

From school or village hall to large professional theatres there are infinite ways to stage this play, but a flexible space where the action can remain fluid, fast moving and continuous is desirable above lots of scenery that would clutter the space and stop the action at any point whenever there is a change of location. A minimal set, able to suggest several locations and allowing flexible staging, is ideal. Many of the scenes require little more than tables, chairs, desks and some carefully focused lighting. Some of the strongest images are of running and flying and a director should bear these qualities in mind in considering the play for production. Run and fly.

It is important that the play takes place on one day from waking up to the scene in the cinema at 11 p.m. as it is this that gives the play a shape and rhythm. The flashback within the classroom also takes place on one day although these scenes should flow effortlessly into each other with the quality of a dream.

The three worlds of the play are home, school and field. Home is Billy, Jud and Mum and is the drama of kitchen sinks. School is a boy lost in a muddle of many others, each vying and hoping for futures out of this existence. It is time-tabled, ordered, with many rules and rituals. And the field is a world of adventure, of flying and of escape. A land without maps or boundaries.

The story is told with a series of choruses – people going to or from work, the chorus of school pupils and Billy's estate world – milkman, newsagents, butchers, chip shop, betting shop. Billy's other chorus is the invisible relay of birds to which he is lead actor. Billy runs through the story and ties the choruses, styles and stories together. He should never leave the stage and the story needs to come to him. Thus, *Kes* is also a journey play. It is a journey, however difficult or problematic, and should flow following our central character.

One of the most frequent questions asked will be 'How are you going to do the bird?' Here is Barry Hines's answer:

Kes is about education not falconry. It's a story about a boy not a bird. I think that's why the novel translates so effectively to the stage. You don't have to see the kestrel to appreciate Billy Casper's troubles. His problems are concerned with family and school. The kestrel is a symbol of Billy's potential. Through the hawk we see what he is capable of, and this element of the play works just as strongly in the imagination as if seen.

I would like to thank all those people who have contributed to this adaptation over ten years – actors, designers, directors, teachers, writers, composers and choreographers. But mostly I pay tribute to the thousands of young people who have found something of themselves in the running and flying of Billy Casper.

Lawrence Till
Watford
February 2000

This adaptation of *Kes* was first performed at the Quarry Theatre, West Yorkshire Playhouse, on 10 April 1999, with the following cast:

MRS CASPER	Joanna Bacon
YOUTH EMPLOYMENT OFFICER, FARMER	Nicholas Camm
MR SUGDEN, MR BEAL	Alan Cowan
MILKMAN, MR FARTHING	Dermot Keaney
JUD	Ian Kelsey
MACDOWALL	Dale Meeks
MR PORTER, MR GRYCE	Frank Moorey
BILLY CASPER	Raymond Pickard
TIBBUT	Edward Price
MRS MACDOWALL, LIBRARIAN, MRS ROSE, MISS FENTON	Sarah Turton

Other parts played by member of the company

Directed by Natasha Betteridge
Designed by Laura Hopkins
Lighting Designer Jon Buswell
Sound Designer Mic Pool

Characters

BILLY CASPER
MRS CASPER
JUD

MR SUGDEN
MR BEAL
MR FARTHING
MR PORTER
MR GRYCE
MACDOWALL
TIBBUT
DELAMORE
GIBBS
YOUTH EMPLOYMENT OFFICER

MILKMAN
FARMER
FARMER'S DAUGHTER
LIBRARIAN
MRS MACDOWALL
MRS ROSE
MISS FENTON

CUSTOMERS
MINERS
PUPILS
SMOKERS
MESSENGER
READERS IN LIBRARY
PUNTERS

ACT ONE

Scene 1

Early Morning Journey to School, 6.00 am

The first scene follows BILLY*'s journey to school. It flows without stopping and with* BILLY *running between the different locations.*

We first see BILLY *and* JUD *together in bed asleep in their bedroom. It is cold and dark and uncomforting. The alarm clock rings.* JUD *rolls over, coughs and fidgets, reaches out of bed, for the alarm clock. It falls from the bedside cabinet.* JUD *sinks back into his pillow.*

JUD. Come here, you bloody thing.

BILLY (*pause*). Jud?

JUD. What?

BILLY. You'd better get up.

    Pause.

    The alarm's gone off you know.

JUD. D'you think I don't know?

    JUD *pulls the blankets round him.*

BILLY. Jud?

JUD. What?

BILLY. You'll be late.

JUD. Shut it.

BILLY. Clock's not fast you know.

JUD. I said 'Shut it'.

    JUD *elbows* BILLY *in the back.*

BILLY. Give over, that hurts!

JUD. Well shut it then.

BILLY. I'll tell me Mum on you.

JUD. Shut your stinking mouth.

> JUD *hits him again in the back.* JUD *sits on the edge of the bed, then gets up and puts the bedroom light on.*

BILLY. Set clock on for me, Jud. For seven.

JUD. Set it yourself.

BILLY. Go on, you're up.

> JUD *pulls the blankets off* BILLY, *stripping the bed completely.* BILLY *has his hands between his legs in an attempt to keep warm.*

JUD. Hands *off* cocks, *on* socks.

BILLY. You rotten sod, just because you've to get up.

JUD. A few weeks lad and you'll be getting up with me.

> JUD *has his trousers on by now and goes to the kitchen to continue dressing.*

BILLY. Switch the light out then!

> JUD *ignores him.* BILLY *lies still a moment then retrieves the blankets after switching off the light.* JUD *in the kitchen, turns on the radio, finds himself some bread and jam, makes his snap and puts it in his tin. He takes his racing paper from his jacket and writes his bet, and begins to make tea.*
>
> BILLY *scratches his hair gets dressed and then joins* JUD, *pulling his mother's jumper on to keep warm.* BILLY *arranges the dirty cups from the night before throughout the following. Unable to get warm he puts on his windcheater. The zip is broken.*

JUD (*writing*). 'Tell Him He's Dead', 2.30 Doncaster. (*Seeing* BILLY.) What's up with you? Shit the bed?

BILLY. Have you seen t' time? You're gonna be late.

JUD. Think I don't know?

BILLY. Is there any tea? (*There isn't.* BILLY *sighs and yawns.*) Smashing morning again.

JUD. You wouldn't be saying that if you were going where I'm going. (*Writing.*) 'Crackpot.' Three o'clock, Newbury.

BILLY. Just think, when I'm doing papers you'll be going down pit in t' cage.

JUD. Another few weeks, lad, and you'll be coming down wi' me.

BILLY. I'll not.

JUD. Won't you?

BILLY. No.

JUD. Why's that?

BILLY. 'Cos I'm not going to work down pit.

JUD. Where you gonna work then?

BILLY. I don't know but I'm not going to work down pit.

JUD. No?

BILLY. No.

JUD. No, and have I to tell you why? For one thing you've to be able to read and write before they'll set you on. And for another, they wouldn't have a weedy little twat like you. You can put this bet on for me. 'Crackpot', 'Tell Him He's Dead'. Here's money.

JUD *hits* BILLY *as he goes out.* BILLY *looks for something to drink. There is nothing.* BILLY *sees* JUD'*s snap tin left on the table, opens it, and begins to eat one of the sandwiches. He is halfway through it when* JUD *returns.*

JUD. I forgot me snap.

He sees BILLY *and makes a dive at him.*

I'll bloody murder you when I get home. And don't bother with your bike – I've already got it.

BILLY *pulls on his shoes, gets rid of his mum's jumper and collects his newspaper bag from under the table. He runs from the house.*

It is still getting light. He passes people getting ready for their day. Postmen, milkmen, two miners coming off the night shift. From here to BILLY*'s arrival at school the stage is populated with people going about the morning rituals which start the day. The action flows continuously.*

We hear a car passing. A shop doorbell rings. We're in MR PORTER*'s paper shop.*

MR PORTER (*arranging newspapers on his counter*). I thought you weren't coming.

BILLY. Why, I'm not late am I?

MR PORTER (*taking out his watch and considering it*). Very near.

BILLY. I nearly was though.

MR PORTER. What do you mean?

BILLY. Late. Our Jud went to pit on me bike.

MR PORTER (*handing* BILLY *newspapers*). What are you going to do then?

BILLY. Walk it.

MR PORTER. Walk it! How long do you think that's going to take you?

BILLY. It'll not take me long.

MR PORTER. Some folks like to read their papers the day they come out.

BILLY. It's not my fault. I didn't ask him to take my bike, did I?

MR PORTER. No and I didn't ask for any cheek from you! Do you hear?

BILLY (*quietly*). Yes.

MR PORTER (*sighing*). There's a waiting list a mile long for your job you know. Grand lads and all, some of 'em. Lads from up Firs Hill and round there.

BILLY *is warming his backside on a heater while* MR PORTER *continues arranging papers.*

BILLY. What's up? It'll not take me that much longer. I've done it before. I know some short cuts.

MR PORTER. Well don't be short cutting over people's property.

BILLY. No, across some fields. It cuts miles off.

MR PORTER. Well be sure the farmer doesn't see you, else you might have a barrel of shot spread up your arse.

BILLY. I haven't let you down yet, have I?

A CUSTOMER *comes into the shop and* MR PORTER *gives him his paper.*

MR PORTER. Morning, sir, not very promising again. Looks like rain.

CUSTOMER. And twenty Players tipped please.

MR PORTER. Right, sir. I've not got twenty. Will two tens do you?

CUSTOMER. Aye.

While MR PORTER *gets the cigarettes and the* CUSTOMER *is leafing through his paper, Billy lifts two bars of chocolate from a display at the side of the counter. He drops them into his newspaper bag as* MR PORTER *turns round to hand over the cigarettes and put the money in the till. This stealing ritual is commonplace for* BILLY.

MR PORTER. I thank you. Good morning, sir.

The CUSTOMER *leaves.* MR PORTER *climbs a ladder to stack shelves.* BILLY *steals more chocolate during the following.*

Next thing you'll be wanting me to deliver 'em for you! You know what they said when I took you on, don't you. They said you'll have to keep your eyes open now, you know, 'cos they're all alike off that estate, up there. They'll steal your breath, if you're not careful.

BILLY. I've never stole nowt of yours, have I?

MR PORTER. I've not given you a chance that's why.

BILLY. You don't have to, I haven't been nicking for ages. I've stopped getting into trouble now.

BILLY *squeezes past* MR PORTER *on a ladder and shakes it on purpose.*

Look out, Mr Porter! Careful!

MR PORTER *sways and loses his balance.*

You're all right. I've got hold of you.

MR PORTER. You clumsy young bugger. What are you trying to do, kill me?

BILLY. I lost me balance, Mr Porter. I must have tripped. I was trying to catch you.

MR PORTER. I wouldn't put it past you either.

BILLY. You wanna watch that ladder, Mr Porter.

MR PORTER *descends the ladder feeling his heart.*

MR PORTER. I fair felt me heart go then.

BILLY. Just sit down here a couple of minutes. Are you all right now, Mr Porter?

MR PORTER (*sitting and looking at his pocket watch*). All right? Aye, I'm bloody champion.

BILLY. You're all right. I wouldn't let you fall.

MR PORTER. Are you going to stand there all day, then? I don't know. I'll have everybody ringing me up and asking why I can't deliver on time.

BILLY. What time is it?

MR PORTER. Time you were at school.

BILLY. Is it that late?

MR PORTER. Them poor teachers. I wouldn't like to try and learn you owt, for all the coal in Barnsley.

BILLY. I'll be off then.

BILLY *runs from the shop.*

MR PORTER. And don't be late for tonight's!

BILLY *begins to deliver papers, eating the chocolate he stole from the shop. We see more people starting their day,*

off to work, off to school. BILLY *takes out* The Dandy.
BILLY *is confident and excited by comics and plays
characters well. The following is fun and animated, but
betrays* BILLY*'s inability to read well.*

BILLY (*reading*). A sneaky ruffian's latest plan means a sticky
problem for Desperate Dan.

Desperate Dan is stronger than all, but this opponent makes
him fall.

Mmm, dinner. But who's this?

Right! Where do you want to fight?

Right here.

S – K – I – I – I – D !

Down I go again. What's making me fall?

Now's my chance to jump on his chest.

T – H – U – D – D – D !

You won't catch me out this time you braggart. You won't
catch me. A sock in the midriff will settle your game.

S – S – S – P – L – A – S – H.

What's this on my face? Why, it's grease. Give me that tube
back. So this is how you've been making me slip! He was
squirting invisible grease under my feet! You dirty twister!
It's time somebody taught you a lesson.

Take T – H – A – A – A – T – T – T ! ! !

C – R – A – S – H ! ! !

Where did he end up?

. . . in t' middle of next week, Uncle Dan.

BILLY *continues delivering papers. The* MILKMAN *enters
whistling and delivering milk. During the following, when*
MILKMAN *is distracted,* BILLY *steals a pint of orange
juice and a carton of eggs from the* MILKMAN*'s carrier.*
BILLY *puts them in his jacket pocket or newspaper bag.*

MILKMAN. How's it going then, young 'un?

BILLY. Oh, not so bad.

MILKMAN. You could do with some transport. Do you fancy a lift? A milk float's better than walking, you know.

BILLY. Ah, only just, though. They only go about five miles an hour, them things.

MILKMAN. It's still better than walking, in't it?

BILLY. I could go faster on a kid's scooter.

MILKMAN. You know what I always say?

BILLY. What?

MILKMAN. Third class riding's better than first class walking any day.

BILLY. I'm not so sure on one of them ramshacks.

MILKMAN. Please yourself. See yer.

BILLY. See yer, mister.

The MILKMAN *delivers milk and exits, whistling.* BILLY *drinks the orange juice. We hear the sound of the milk cart moving away.*

The pit hooter sounds. BILLY *runs home to . . .*

MRS CASPER *is getting dressed and making-up in the kitchen mirror.* BILLY *puts orange on table and throws his newspaper bag under the table, transferring the carton of eggs to his jacket. He has seen a man leaving the front door as he entered the back.*

MRS CASPER. Is that you, Reg? Oh, it's you, Billy. Haven't you gone to school yet?

BILLY (*looking off*). Who's that bloke?

MRS CASPER. That's Reg. You know Reg, don't you?

BILLY. Is that him you came home with last night? Reg?

MRS CASPER. Oh, shut up, Billy. I've not much time. I'm gonna be late for work again. There's some tea mashed if you want a cup. I don't know if the milk's come or not.

BILLY. Was it?

MRS CASPER. Oh, stop pestering me. I've not much time. I've got to get to work. You got a fag?

BILLY. No. Was it?

MRS CASPER. Do me a favour love, and run up to t' shop for some fags.

BILLY. Old Porter won't give you owt, he says.

MRS CASPER. Go along to Hardy's then love. He gives us tick.

BILLY. That's miles and he'll not be open yet.

MRS CASPER. You can go to the back door, Mr Hardy'll not mind.

BILLY (*putting on his school tie*). I can't, I'll be late.

MRS CASPER. Go on love. And bring a few things back with you, a loaf, some butter, a few eggs, summat like that. We can have some breakfast then.

BILLY. Go yourself.

MRS CASPER. I've not much time. I need a fag. Tell him to put it int' book and I'll pay him at weekend.

BILLY. He says you can't have owt else 'til you've paid up.

MRS CASPER. He always says that. Ignore him. Tell him I'll come and see him tonight after work. Tell him that. I'll give you summat if you go. And there's a bet of our Jud's to take to t' bookies. Don't forget that.

BILLY. I'm not taking it.

MRS CASPER. You'd better had, lad.

BILLY. I'm fed up of taking bets every day. Why can't he take 'em?

MRS CASPER. How can he, you dozy bugger, when he's down pit all that time? He don't finish 'til races is over.

BILLY. I don't care, I'm not taking it. I'll be late.

BILLY *makes for the door, but* MRS CASPER *blocks his way.*

MRS CASPER. Billy, get up to them shops and do as you're told.

BILLY. Go yourself.

> MRS CASPER *swipes at him, and misses.* BILLY *moves behind the table.*

MRS CASPER. You cheeky young bugger.

BILLY. Give over now, mum, I'll be late for school.

MRS CASPER. You'll be more than late, unless you do as you're told.

BILLY. Gryce said I'd get stick next time I'm late.

MRS CASPER. That's nowt to what you'll get if I catch you. And I'll catch you, my lad. Don't you believe it.

> BILLY *pretends to go one way,* MRS CASPER *grabs at him as he goes the other way and out of the door into the garden, over the fence and into the fields.*

Just you wait 'til tonight. And you'd better place that bet. Jud'll kill you if you forget. Just you wait, you'll see.

> BILLY *takes out the carton of eggs and throws them at the side of the house one by one.*

And don't think *I've* forgotten lad 'cos I haven't. Just you wait, lad, 'til I get home tonight.

> BILLY *gives her the V sign and runs to . . .*

Scene 2

School Assembly, 9.00 am

The school bell rings. MR CROSSLEY *is marking his class register as everyone groups for assembly in the school hall. There is a raised area with a lectern and microphone. Extend the register as required until the stage is filled with* PUPILS.

MR CROSSLEY. Abbott.

PUPIL. Sir.

MR CROSSLEY. Anderson.

PUPIL. Sir.

MR CROSSLEY Arkwright.

PUPIL. Sir.

MR CROSSLEY. Bath.

PUPIL. Away, Sir.

MR CROSSLEY. Bennett.

PUPIL. Sir.

MR CROSSLEY. Bridges.

PUPIL. Yes, Sir.

MR CROSSLEY. Brinkman.

PUPIL. Sir.

MR CROSSLEY. Casper.

PUPIL. Sir.

MR CROSSLEY. Daintry.

PUPIL. Sir.

MR CROSSLEY. Ellis.

PUPIL. Sir.

MR CROSSLEY. Fisher.

BILLY. German Bight.

MR CROSSLEY (*has marked his register before he realises what* BILLY *has said*). What was that?

PUPILS. It was Casper, sir / Mr Crossley / He's crackers, sir / He can't help it.

MR CROSSLEY. Did you say something, Casper?

BILLY. Yes, sir, I didn't . . .

MR CROSSLEY. Now then Casper. What did you say?

BILLY. German Bight, sir.

The PUPILS *laugh.*

MR CROSSLEY. Silence. Is this your feeble idea of a joke, Casper?

BILLY. No, sir.

MR CROSSLEY. Well what was the idea then?

BILLY. I don't know, sir. It was when you said Fisher. It just came out: Fisher – German Bight. It's the shipping forecast, sir. German Bight comes after Fisher. Fisher, German Bight, Cromarty. I know 'em all. I listen to it every night. I like to hear t' names.

MR CROSSLEY. And you thought you'd enlighten me and the school with your idiotic information?

BILLY. No, sir.

MR CROSSLEY. Blurting out and making a mess of my register.

BILLY. It just come out, sir.

MR CROSSLEY. And so did you, Casper. Just come out from under a stone.

The PUPILS *laugh.*

Quiet!

The Headmaster, MR GRYCE, *comes onto the platform and the* PUPILS *immediately go quiet. He commands absolute respect from everyone. The school music group with their assorted instruments, led by* MISS FENTON *position themselves to one side.*

MR GRYCE. God's in his Heaven. All's right with the world. Hymn number 175. 'New Every Morning is the Love'.

The music strikes up. It is accurate but unmusical and the choice of instruments inappropriate. The song is punctuated with much fidgeting, passing of notes and behaviour unseen by the teachers. This Hymn should be cut to fit the action.

ALL (*sing*).
New every morning is the love.
Our wakening and uprising prove;
Through sleep and darkness safely brought,
Restored to life, and power, and thought.

New mercies, each returning day,
Hover around us while we pray;
New perils past, new sins forgiven,
New thoughts of God, new hopes of heaven.

MR GRYCE. Stop! And what is that *noise* supposed to represent? Miss Fenton I am very disappointed. I've heard sweeter sounds coming from a slaughter-house! This is supposed to be a hymn of joy – not a dirge. The whole school will therefore return to this hall after school is over. Then you'll sing. Or I'll *make* you sing like you've never sung before. Now, with joy!

ALL (*sing*). If on our daily course our mind
　　　Be set to hallow all we find
　　　New treasures still, of countless price,
　　　God will provide for sacrifice.

　　　Old friends, old scenes, will lovelier be,
　　　As more of Heaven in each we see;
　　　Some softening gleam of love and prayer
　　　Will dawn on every cross and care.

　　　The trivial round, the common task,
　　　Will furnish all we ought to ask;
　　　Room to deny ourselves; a road
　　　To bring us daily nearer God.

　　　Only, O Lord, in Thy dear love
　　　Fit us for perfect rest above;
　　　And help us, this and every day,
　　　To live more nearly as we pray.

GIRL (*falteringly*). This morning's reading is taken from Saint Matthew Eighteen. Never despise one of these little ones. I tell you they have their Guardian Angels in Heaven who look continually on the face of me Heavenly Father.

The pupils gradually begin coughing through the next paragraph. One person. Silence. Then three. Seven. More and more.

Suppose a man has hundred sheep if one of 'em strays does he not leave the other ninety-nine on the hillside and go in search of the one that strayed . . . the one that strayed . . . (*She gives up.*)

MR GRYCE. Stop that infernal coughing! It's every morning alike. As soon as *one* starts you're *all* off. It's more like a dirt track than an Assembly Hall.

Pause. Silence. Then, a lone cough near MACDOWALL, *but clearly enough to be not him.*

Who did that? I said, who did that? (*No one owns up.*) Mr Sugden. Somewhere near you. Didn't you see the boy?

MR SUGDEN *pushes his way into the lines of* PUPILS.

There Sugden! That's where it came from! Around there!

MR SUGDEN *grabs hold of* MACDOWALL.

MACDOWALL. It wan't me, sir.

MR SUGDEN. Of course it was you.

MACDOWALL. It wasn't, sir. Honest.

MR SUGDEN. Don't argue lad, I saw you.

MR GRYCE. MacDowall. I might have known it. Report to my office after assembly and Heaven help you. Right, carry on, girl.

GIRL (*Even more faltering and anxious now*) . . . and go in search of the one that strayed. And if he should find it I tell you your Heavenly Father is more delighted over that sheep that strayed . . . (*She loses her place.*) . . . that sheep that strayed than over the ninety-nine that never strayed. Here ends this morning's reading.

MR GRYCE. Very good, girl. Now sit.

All the PUPILS *sit, except the daydreaming* BILLY *who remains standing.*

There will be a meeting . . . Casper! Casper!

BILLY *opens his eyes and sits down.*

Up Casper! Up on your feet, lad.

The PUPILS *are riotous.*

Silence! Unless some of you want to stand up with him. (*To* BILLY.) And get your head up, lad! Or you'll be falling asleep again. You were asleep weren't you? Well? Speak up, lad!

BILLY. I don't know, sir.

MR GRYCE. Well I know. You were fast asleep on your feet. Weren't you?

BILLY. Yes, sir.

MR GRYCE. Fast asleep during the Gospel reading! You irreligious boy! Were you tired, lad?

BILLY. I don't know, sir.

MR GRYCE. Don't know? You wouldn't be tired if you'd get to bed at night instead of roaming the streets at all hours up to mischief.

BILLY. No, sir.

MR GRYCE. Or sitting up 'til dawn watching some tripe on television. Report to my room straight after assembly. You'll be tired when I've finished with you, lad. Sit.

BILLY *sits.*

There will be a meeting of the intermediate football team in the gym at break this morning. Later this week, we will be privileged to have with us the *Opera for All* Company, whose performance I am sure you are all looking forward to with great anticipation. *Opera for All* is a touring company that visits schools and other institutions to give you the unique opportunity to experience live opera. Perhaps this will open the door to a life-long love of opera. Who knows. At the end of the performance you will show your appreciation in the usual manner. That means no whistling, stamping or yelling.

A reminder that the Youth Employment Officer will be in this afternoon to see the Easter leavers. They will be sent for from their respective classes and should report to the medical room, where the interviews will take place. Your parents *should* have been told by this time, but if any pupil *has* forgotten and thinks that their parents may wish to attend the interview, then they can consult the list on the main notice board for approximate times. I would also like to see the three members of the smokers' union whom I didn't have time to deal with yesterday. They can pay their dues at my room straight after assembly.

The school bell rings. The PUPILS *become restless.* MR GRYCE *stops them in their tracks.*

That bell is for my benefit, not for you. (*Pause.*) Right, dismissed.

Scene 3

Outside Mr Gryce's Office, 9.25 am

MACDOWALL, BILLY, DELAMORE *and two other* SMOKERS *remain on stage waiting for* MR GRYCE.

MACDOWALL. It's his favourite trick this. He likes to keep you waiting. He thinks it makes it worse.

DELAMORE. Don't worry, MacDowall, you've got the opera to look forward to. (*Sings operatically.*) HA HA HA.

SMOKER 1 (*sings*). HA HA HA.

DELAMORE (*sings*). WILLIAM?

SMOKER 1 (*sings*). WHAT, PHILIP?

DELAMORE (*sings*). DO YOU LOVE ME?

SMOKER 1 (*sings*). DO I BOLLOCKS.

DELAMORE (*sings*). OH, WILLIAM I THOUGHT THAT YOU DID.

SMOKER 1 (*sings*). I NEVER SAID SO. NO. NO. NO.

DELAMORE (*sings*). YOU ROTTEN SWINE. YOU'VE BROKEN ME HEART.

SMOKER 2 (*sings*). IT SERVES YOU RIGHT. HA HA HA. HA HA HA.

BOTH (*sings*). HA HA HA.

OTHERS (*sings*). HA HA HA.

MACDOWALL. Ha, ha-bloody-ha. It wan't me that coughed you know. I'm going to tell Gryce that an' all.

DELAMORE. It makes no difference whether you tell him or not, he doesn't listen.

MACDOWALL. I'll bring me Dad up if he gives me stick.

BILLY. What you always bringing your Dad up for? He never does owt when he comes. They say last time your Dad came up, Gryce gave him t' stick an' all.

MACDOWALL. At least I've got a proper Dad to bring up. That's more than you can say, Casper. Where's your Dad then?

BILLY. Shut your gob, MacDowall.

MACDOWALL. Why, what are you going to do about it?

BILLY. You'd be surprised.

MACDOWALL. Right then, I'll see you at dinner.

BILLY. Anytime you want.

MACDOWALL. Right then.

BILLY. Right then.

Pause. A MESSENGER *enters with a note for* MR GRYCE. *He is the most innocent looking boy in the school.*

DELAMORE. If you've come for t' stick you'd better get to t' back of queue.

MESSENGER. I've not come for the stick. Mr Crossley sent me with a message for Mr Gryce.

MACDOWALL (*taking his cigarettes out of his pocket and going to the* MESSENGER). You'd better save us these 'til after. If he searches us he'll only take 'em off us and give us another two strokes. Here.

MESSENGER. I don't want 'em, you're not getting me into trouble as well.

MACDOWALL. Who's getting you into trouble? You can give 'em us back after.

MESSENGER (*shaking his head*). I don't want 'em.

MACDOWALL (*threatening the young boy*). Do you want some fist instead?

They surround the MESSENGER *and fill his pockets with their cigarettes, matches and lighters.*

DELAMORE (*sings*). I THINK I WILL GO TO T' BOG
NOW.

SMOKER 1 (*sings*). A VERY GOOD IDEA, DELA – MORE
– MORE – MORE!

DELAMORE (*sings*). ARE YOU COMING W-I-T-H ME-E-E-E?

SMOKER 1 (*sings*). NO-O I DO NOT THINK SO. NO NO
NO!

DELAMORE (*sings*). WHY NO-OT? WHY NO-OT?

SMOKER 1. Because Gryce Pudding is coming.

MR GRYCE *approaches to investigate the noise.*

MR GRYCE. What's going on here?

DELAMORE. Nowt, sir.

SMOKER 2. What, sir?

MR GRYCE. 'What, sir?' Singing, laughing, making a
mockery in the corridor. What were you laughing at, boy?

DELAMORE. Nothing, sir.

MR GRYCE. Nothing? Nothing? They lock people up for
laughing at nothing.

MESSENGER. Please, sir.

MR GRYCE. Don't interrupt boy, when I'm speaking.

Look at you. You've got the world on a plate. You know it
all, you young people, don't you? With your gear and your
music. Nobody can tell you anything, can they? But it's
only superficial. Just a sheen with nothing worthwhile or
solid underneath. There's something happening today that's
frightening, that makes me feel that it's all been a waste of
time.

MESSENGER. Please, sir.

MR GRYCE. Don't interrupt, boy. I won't tell you again. A
waste of time. Like it's a waste of time me standing here
talking to you boys, because you won't take a blind bit of
notice of what I'm saying. I know what you're thinking
now. You're thinking why doesn't he just get on with it

instead of standing there babbling on. That's what you're thinking isn't it? Isn't it MacDowall?

MACDOWALL. No, sir.

MR GRYCE. Oh, yes it is. I can see it in your eyes lad, they're glazed over. You're not interested. Now, in the old days we bred people with respect. We knew where we stood in those days. Even today a man will stop me in the street and say 'Hello, Mr Gryce, remember me?' And we'll pass the time of day and chat, and he'll laugh about the thrashings I gave him. But what do I get from you lot? A honk from a greasy pimply faced youth behind the wheel of some big second-hand car. Or an obscene remark from a gang *after* they've passed me.

And do you know how I know all this?

MR GRYCE *reveals his cane.*

Because I still have to use this every day. It's fantastic isn't it, that in this day and age, in this super-scientific, all-things-bright-and-beautiful age, that the only way of running this school efficiently is by the rule of the cane. But why? There should be no need of it now.

So, for want of a better solution I continue to use this, knowing full well that you'll be back time after time and time and time again for some more. Knowing that when you smokers leave this room wringing your hands, you'll carry on smoking just the same. Yes, you can smirk, lad. I'll bet your pockets are loaded up at this very moment in readiness for break, aren't they? Aren't they? Well just empty them. Come on all of you. Empty your pockets!

The SMOKERS, BILLY *and* MACDOWALL *begin to empty their pockets.*

MESSENGER. Please, sir.

MR GRYCE. You again? Quiet lad and get your pockets emptied.

He moves along the line of boys inspecting the contents of their pockets.

This can't be true, I don't believe it. Keep your hands out.

He goes along the line again frisking their clothing. He knows the tricks and finally comes to the young MESSENGER. MR GRYCE *searches his pockets.*

Aah!

MESSENGER. Please, sir.

MR GRYCE *empties the* MESSENGER*'s pockets.*

MR GRYCE. A regular little cigarette-factory aren't you?

MESSENGER. Please, sir.

MR GRYCE. You didn't think you could get away with a weak trick like that did you? (*To the others.*) Now get that other junk into your pockets and all of you get your hands out.

They step forward one by one and are caned on each hand. Finally the MESSENGER *is caned. We focus on him whilst we set up . . .*

Scene 4

English Class, 10.00 am

PUPILS *enter, forming the classroom with desks and chairs around the* SMOKERS, BILLY *and* MACDOWALL.

MR FARTHING *is taking the class for English. On the blackboard is written Fact and Fiction.*

MR FARTHING. Right 4C: Fiction. Whitbread, look up 'fiction' in your dictionary.

WHITBREAD (*reading*). *Fiction: invented statement or narrative, novels, stories, collectiv, collectiv-ly, collectively, con . . . con . . .* Blimey.

MR FARTHING. Go on, have a go.

WHITBREAD. *Con . . . vent, con . . . vent . . . ion . . . ally,* I know, *conventionally accepted falsehood. Fic-ti-tious: not genuine, imaginary, assumed.*

MR FARTHING (*taking the dictionary and reading*). *Invented statement or narrative, novels, stories, collectively conventionally accepted falsehood. Fictitious: not genuine, imaginary, assumed.* And we call all this?

PUPILS. Fiction, sir.

MR FARTHING. Right, fiction. Now then 4C, what's the opposite of fiction? What do we call things that are real?

PUPILS. Facts, sir.

MR FARTHING. Facts. And tell me what a fact is. Don't give a fact. Don't say that Barraclough's got a snotty-nose or anything like that.

PUPIL 1. Fact is summat you find out, sir.

PUPIL 2. It's another word for t' truth, Mr Farthing.

MR FARTHING. Right, something that has happened. Something that we know is real. Things that we read about in newspapers or hear on the news. Events, accidents, meetings; the things that we see with our own eyes. All these are facts. Have you got that?

PUPILS. Yes, sir.

MR FARTHING. Right then. Now if I asked Anderson for some facts about himself what could he tell us?

PUPILS. Sir! Sir!

MR FARTHING. All right! All right. Just put your hands up. There's no need to jump down my throat.

PUPIL 3. He's wearing trousers, Mr Farthing.

MR FARTHING. Good.

PUPIL 4. He's got lovely brown hair and blue eyes, sir.

PUPILS. Whooo!

MR FARTHING. Yes, Armitage?

PUPIL 5. He lives down Shallowbank Crescent.

MR FARTHING. Do you Anderson?

ANDERSON. Yes, sir.

MR FARTHING. Good.

TIBBUT. He smokes, sir.

ANDERSON. Do I nick, Tibbut?

TIBBUT. You do.

ANDERSON. Get knotted.

MR FARTHING. All right, all right, I'm not interested in what he does, out of school hours as long as he doesn't come into class smoking a fag. Right then, now all these are facts about Anderson but they're not particularly interesting facts. Perhaps Anderson can tell us something about himself that is interesting. A *really* interesting fact.

PUPILS (*picking up on something sordid or sexual*). Woooo!

MR FARTHING. Quietly now. Quietly!

ANDERSON. I don't know owt, sir.

MR FARTHING. Anything at all, Anderson. Something that's happened to you, which sticks in your mind. What about when you were little?

ANDERSON. There's summat, but it's nowt though, sir.

MR FARTHING. It must be interesting if you remember it.

ANDERSON. It was a joke really.

MR FARTHING. Well tell us, and we'll all have a laugh, then.

ANDERSON. Well, it was when I was a kid. I was at Junior School, I think, or somewhere like that, and we went down to Fowler's Pond, me and this other kid. Reggie Clay they called him. He didn't come to this school. He and his family did a flit and went away somewhere. Anyway, it was Spring, tadpole time, and it was swarming with tadpoles there in the Spring. The edges of the Pond were black with 'em, and me and Reggie started to catch 'em. It was easy. All you did was put your hands together and scoop a handful of water and you'd got a handful of tadpoles.

Anyway we were mucking about with 'em, picking 'em up and chucking 'em back in t' pond and things, and we were on about taking some home, but we'd no jam jars. So this kid, Reggie, says, 'Take your wellingtons off and put some in there. They'll be all right till we get home.' So, I take 'em off and put water in 'em and I says to this kid 'Let's have a competition, you have one wellington and I'll have t' other, and we'll see who can get most in.' So he starts to fill one wellington and I start to fill t' other. We must have been at it for hours, and they get thicker and thicker, until at the end there was no water left in 'em, they're just jam-packed with tadpoles.

You ought to have seen 'em, all black and shining, right up to t' top. When we'd finished we dipped our fingers into 'em and kept whipping 'em at each other, all shouting and excited like. Then this kid says to me 'I bet you daren't put one on.' And I says, 'I bet *you* daren't.' So, we say we'll *both* put one on. We wouldn't though. We kept reckoning to, then running away. So we toss a coin and him who lost has to do it first. And I lost. And, oh, and you'd to take your socks off as well. That were part of the dare. So, I take me socks off, and I'm looking at this wellington full of tadpoles, and this kid keeps saying 'Go on then. You're frightened. You're frightened.' I was an' all.

Anyway I shut my eyes and start to put one foot in t' live jelly. They're freezing cold. And my foot goes right down and they all come over t' top of my wellington and as I get my foot to t' bottom I can feel 'em all squashing about between my toes. Anyway, I've done it, and I says to this kid 'You put yourn on now.' But he won't. He's dead scared. So I put it on instead. I'd got used to it by then. It's all right after a bit. It sends your legs all exciting and tingly like. When I get 'em both on I walk up to this kid, waving my arms and making spook noises. And as I walk the tadpoles all come squelching over the tops again and run down t' sides. This kid looks frightened to death. He keeps looking down at my wellingtons so I run at him and they all spurt up my legs. You ought to see him. He just screams out and runs skriking home. When he'd gone it was the funniest feeling. Standing there, all quiet, with nobody else, up to my knees in tadpoles.

Pause.

MR FARTHING. Very good, Anderson. Thank you. Now has anyone else got anything interesting to tell us?

No hands go up. BILLY *is fidgeting, his hands still stinging from the caning.* MR FARTHING *notices him.*

What about you, Casper?

BILLY *does not hear him. The* PUPILS *are amused by these regular incidents.*

Casper! Stand up!

BILLY. What, sir?

MR FARTHING. What, sir? You'd know if you'd been listening.

BILLY. Yes, sir.

MR FARTHING. What have we been talking about?

BILLY. Er. Stories, sir.

MR FARTHING. What kind of stories?

BILLY. Er.

MR FARTHING. You don't know do you? You haven't been listening to a word I've said, have you?

TIBBUT. He's been asleep again, sir.

BILLY. Shut your mouth, Tibbut.

MR FARTHING. Casper. Tibbut. You'll both be asleep in a minute. I'll knock you to sleep. The rest of you quiet.

PUPILS *are quiet.*

Right, Casper you can do some work for a change. You're going to tell us some facts about yourself.

BILLY. I don't know any, sir.

MR FARTHING. Well, you can just stand there until you do. There's always someone who has to be awkward, who refuses to be interested in anything, someone like you, Casper.

I'll give you two minutes to think of something, lad, and if you haven't started then the whole class is coming back at four o'clock.

Immediate reaction from the PUPILS. *Various* PUPILS *shout out. Others grumble.*

PUPIL 6. Come on, Billy.

PUPIL 7. Or else you're dead.

PUPIL 8. Say owt.

TIBBUT. If I've to come back I'll kill him.

MR FARTHING. I'm waiting, Casper. (*Pause*) We haven't got all day, Casper.

PUPIL 9. Tell him about your hawk, Casper.

MR FARTHING. If anyone else calls out it will be the last call they'll make. What hawk, Casper? Casper, I'm speaking to you. And stop sulking. Just because somebody says a few words to you. Now then, about this hawk . . . is it a stuffed one?

PUPILS *laugh.*

What's funny about that? Well, Tibbut?

TIBBUT. He's got a hawk, sir. It's a kestrel. He's mad about it. He never knocks about with anybody else now. He just looks after this hawk. He's crackers about it. He goes mad if you say owt about it.

BILLY. It's better than you anyroad –

MR FARTHING *sits. Pause.*

MR FARTHING. All right, Casper. Tell us about this hawk. Where did you get it from?

BILLY *is looking down at his desk.* BILLY *really doesn't want to reveal anything about Kes.*

MR FARTHING. Casper, I'm speaking to you.

Pause.

Look at me boy when I'm speaking to you. Now then, Casper, this hawk.

BILLY. I found it.

MR FARTHING (*gently*). Where?

BILLY. In t' woods.

MR FARTHING. Was it injured? What had happened to it?

BILLY. It was a young-un. It must have fallen from its nest.

MR FARTHING. And how long have you had it?

BILLY. Since last year.

MR FARTHING. All that time. And where do you keep it?

BILLY. In t' shed.

MR FARTHING. And what do you feed it on?

BILLY. Beef. Mice. Birds.

MR FARTHING. Isn't it cruel though, keeping it in a shed all the time? Wouldn't it be happier flying free?

BILLY *looks at* MR FARTHING *for the first time. Pause.*

BILLY. I don't keep it in t' shed all the time. I fly it every day.

MR FARTHING. But doesn't it fly away? I thought hawks were wild birds.

BILLY. 'Course it doesn't fly away. I've trained it.

PUPILS *are amused and unbelieving.*

MR FARTHING. Trained it? I thought you'd to be an expert to train hawks.

BILLY. Well, I did it.

MR FARTHING. Wasn't that difficult?

BILLY. 'Course it were. You've got to be right patient with 'em and take your time.

MR FARTHING. Tell me how you did it then. I've never met a falconer before, I must be in select company.

BILLY (*slowly at fist, gradually gaining confidence*). Well, what you do is, you train 'em through their stomachs. You can only do owt with 'em when they're hungry, so you do all your training at feeding time. I started training Kes after I'd had her about a fortnight. You cut their food down, until you go in one time and they're keen. I could tell with Kes because she jumped straight on me glove as I held it towards her. So while she was feeding I got hold of her jesses and –

MR FARTHING. Her what?

BILLY. Jesses.

MR FARTHING. And how do you spell that, Casper?

BILLY (*to* MR FARTHING *who writes on the blackboard*).
J-E-S-S-E-S.

MR FARTHING (*sits at* BILLY'S *desk in the classroom*). And
what are Jesses, Billy?

BILLY. They're little leather straps that you fasten round
her legs. She wears these all t' time, and you get hold of
'em when she sits on your glove. You push your swivel
through –

MR FARTHING. Whoa! Whoa! You'd better come out here
and give us a demonstration. We're not all experts you
know.

BILLY. Well, when she stands on your fist, you pull her jesses
down between your fingers. Jesses have slits in them like
button-holes on braces. Then you get your swivel, like a
swivel on a dog lead, press both jesses together, and push
ring through, just like fastening a button.

So, now you can try feeding her outside and getting her
used to things, making her jump onto your glove for t' meat.
A reward like. When she's done this a bit you attach a
creance – that's a long line – I used a fishing line. Then you
put t' hawk down on t' fence post. Then you walk into t'
middle of t' field unwinding t' creance – it's so it can't fly
away you see – and t' hawk's waiting for you to stop and
hold your glove up.

MR FARTHING. It sounds exciting.

BILLY. It is. But the best time was when I found her for t' first
time. You ought to have been there then.

MR FARTHING (*to the* PUPILS). Do you want to hear about it?

PUPILS. Yes, sir.

MR FARTHING. Okay, Casper. Carry on.

*The stage is filled with the dappled light of a woodland in
early morning.* BILLY *uses the desks to climb over, under
and round. They become his journey to . . .*

Scene 5

One Year Earlier. Nesting. Early Morning

BILLY *is throwing stones at the window of* MACDOWALL'*s house. A dog barks some way off.*

BILLY (*calling*). Mac. Mac.

    MRS MACDOWALL *comes to the window and leans out. She pulls her dressing-gown tight against the cold.*

BILLY. Is he up?

MRS MACDOWALL. What the bloody hell do you want at this time of t' morning? It's before seven.

BILLLY. Is your Mac up?

MRS MACDOWALL. Of course he's not up. This time on a Saturday?

BILLY. Isn't he getting up?

MRS MACDOWALL. Not that I know of. He's fast asleep.

BILLY. He's a right 'un. We're going bird nesting. Tibby, Mac and me. It was his idea. It was him that planned it an' all. Tibby's cried off an' all. Don't say your Mac's . . .

MRS MACDOWALL. Stop shouting will you? Do you want all t' neighbours up?

BILLY. He's not coming then?

MRS MACDOWALL. No, he's not. You'd better come back after breakfast if you want to see him. Now bugger off.

    She closes the window. BILLY *throws a handful of dirt at it and* MRS MACDOWALL *reappears.*

Bugger off you little sod!

    BILLY *goes bird nesting alone. He continues climbing up over and round the classroom desks. The* PUPILS *watch with interest as a covey of partridges flies up nearby.* BILLY *throws stones after them. He startles a blackbird. The sun begins to rise and there is soon the continuous relay of birdsong.* BILLY *plunges into the undergrowth and*

*cuts and trims a sapling to use as a stick and a sword and
walks on to the woods. He sees a kestrel fly out from a
crevice in the old monastery wall. He follows the progress
of the bird as do all the* PUPILS. BILLY *starts to climb a
wall. When he is a good way up a* FARMER *enters with his
six-year-old* DAUGHTER. *They see* BILLY.

FARMER. What are you doing?

BILLY. Nowt.

FARMER. Well bugger off then, don't you know this is private
property?

BILLY. Can I get up to that kestrel's nest?

FARMER. What kestrel's nest?

BILLY. Up that wall.

FARMER. There's no nest up there so off you go.

BILLY. There is, I've seen it fly in and come out.

FARMER. And what are you going to do when you get up to
it, take all its eggs?

BILLY. There's no eggs in it, they're young-uns.

FARMER. Well there's nowt to go up for then, is there?

BILLY. I just wanted to look, that's all.

FARMER. Yes, and you'll be looking from six feet under if
you tried to climb up there.

BILLY. Has anybody ever been up that wall to look?

FARMER. Not that I know of. It's dangerous. That's why I
won't let her play here. They've been going to pull it down
for ages.

BILLY. I bet I could get up there.

FARMER. You're not going to have the chance though.

BILLY. I just want to look that's all. (*Pause.*) Can I have a look
from t' bottom then? Go on, I've never found a kestrel's
nest before. That's where it is look, in that hole in t' side of
that window. I've been watching it from across in t' wood.
You ought to have seen it, mister, it was smashing.

FARMER (*softening*). Come on, then.

BILLY and the FARMER *address the nest.*

BILLY. That's where it is.

FARMER. I know it is. It's nested here for donkey's years now.

BILLY. Just think, and I never knew.

FARMER. There's not many that does. I see her every day. She'll fly out and then always sit there on that post.

BILLY. Her?

FARMER. That kestrel's a she. Her young 'uns are in t' nest. She collects food for 'em.

BILLY. She's a beauty. I wish I could see her every day. If I lived here I'd get a young 'un and train it.

FARMER. Would you?

BILLY. You can train 'em, you know.

FARMER. And how would you go about that?

BILLY. Do you know?

FARMER. No. And there's not many that does. If they can't be kept properly it's criminal.

BILLY. Do you know anyone what's kept 'em?

FARMER. One or two but they've always let 'em go because they couldn't do owt with 'em. They never seemed to get tame like other birds.

BILLY. Where could I find out about 'em then?

FARMER. I don't know. Books I suppose. I should think there are books on falconry.

The LIBRARIAN *enters. The desks of the classroom become the library tables. The* PUPILS *take out books and become the* READERS *in the library.*

LIBRARIAN. Can I help you?

BILLY. Books on hawks?

LIBRARIAN. Hawks?

BILLY. Where would I get one?

LIBRARIAN. Hawks?

FARMER. You could try Prior's Bookshop or there's the City Library.

BILLY. Yeah, I want a book on falconry.

FARMER. They've books on everything there.

Scene 6

Flashback. The Library. Afternoon

The Library is filled with avid READERS.

LIBRARIAN. I'm not really sure. You'd better try Ornithology.

BILLY. What's that?

LIBRARIAN. In the factual section under Zoology.

The LIBRARIAN *points the way.* BILLY *finds the book and struggles to read.*

BILLY. An Eagle for an Emperor, a Gryfalcon for a King; a Peregrine for a Prince, a Saker for a Knight, a Merlin for a Lady; a Goshawk for a Yeoman, a Sparrowhawk for a Priest, a Musket for a Holy-Water Clerk, a Kestrel for a Knave.

BILLY *returns to the desk.*

LIBRARIAN. Are you a member?

BILLY. What do you mean?

LIBRARIAN. Are you a member of the Library?

BILLY. I don't know about that. I just want to lend this book on falconry that's all.

LIBRARIAN. You can't *borrow* a book unless you're a member. You have to be a member to take a book out.

BILLY. I only want one.

LIBRARIAN. Have you ever filled out one of these forms?

The LIBRARIAN *shows* BILLY *the application form.*

BILLY. No.

LIBRARIAN. Well you're not a member then. Do you live in the Borough?

BILLY. What do you mean?

LIBRARIAN. The Borough. The City.

BILLY. No, I live out on t' Valley Estate.

READERS. Ssh!

LIBRARIAN. Well that's in the Borough, isn't it?

BILLY. Can I get this book out then?

LIBRARIAN. You'll have to take one of these forms home first for your father to sign.

BILLY. Me Dad's away.

LIBRARIAN. You'll have to wait 'til he comes home then.

BILLY. I don't mean away like that. I mean he's left home.

LIBRARIAN. Oh, I see. Well, in that case your mother'll have to sign it.

BILLY. She's at work.

LIBRARIAN. She can sign it when she comes home, can't she?

BILLY. She'll not be home 'til teatime and it's Sunday tomorrow. I want this book today.

READERS. Ssh!

LIBRARIAN. There's no rush is there?

BILLY. Me Mum knows one of the people what works here, that'll help won't it.

LIBRARIAN. No, that doesn't help at all, you still have to have the form signed.

READERS. Ssh!

BILLY. I've never broke a book you know. Haven't tore it or . . .

LIBRARIAN. But look at your hands, they're absolutely filthy. We'll end up with dirty books that way.

BILLY. I don't read dirty books.

LIBRARIAN. I should hope you don't read dirty books. You're not old enough to read dirty books.

BILLY. Can I just sit down at a table and read it then? I'll bring this paper back on Monday then.

LIBRARIAN. No, you can't, you're not a member.

BILLY. Nobody'll know.

LIBRARIAN. It's against the rules.

READERS. Ssh!

Another READER *hands a book to the* LIBRARIAN *to be stamped out. They chat pleasantly about the weather.*
BILLY *puts the book under his jacket and quickly leaves the library. The* PUPILS *leave, leaving just a row of desks for . . .*

JUD. What' you want this for when you can't read?

BILLY. Thanks, missus. I'll bring this paper back on Monday.

Scene 7

Flashback. Billy's House. Evening

JUD *has already entered in his vest and snatched the stolen book from* BILLY*'s hand as he reads it.* READERS *in the Library have left. Some desks still remain.*

BILLY. Gis it here. Come here.

JUD *holds* BILLY *off at arms-length.*

JUD. Falconry? What do you know about falconry?

BILLY. Gis it back.

JUD *pushes* BILLY *onto the settee and examines the book.*

JUD. *A Falconer's Handbook.* Where've you got this from?

BILLY. I've lent it.

JUD. Nicked it more like. Where've you got it from?

BILLY. The Library in town.

JUD. You must be crackers.

BILLY. How do you mean?

JUD. Nicking books. I could understand it if it were money, but chuff me, not a book.

They struggle with the book. JUD *throws it up in the air several times and then across the floor.* BILLY *races around in circles trying to capture the book.* JUD *continues getting dressed.* BILLY *copies sections of the book into his exercise book.*

JUD. Up! Up! Up! Here, have it.

BILLY. Look what you've done now. I'm trying to look after this book.

JUD. Anybody'd think it were treasure you'd got.

BILLY. I've been reading it all afternoon. I'm nearly half-way through. I know lots about 'em already.

JUD. And what better off will you be when you've read it?

BILLY. A lot, 'cos I'm going to get a young kestrel and train it.

JUD. Train it, you couldn't train a flea! (JUD *laughs*.) Anyroad, where you going to get a kestrel from?

BILLY. I know a nest.

JUD. You don't.

BILLY. All right then, I don't.

JUD. Where?

BILLY. I'm not telling.

JUD. I said, *where*?

JUD *jumps astride* BILLY *on the sofa, pushes his face into the cushion, and forces one arm up into a half-nelson.*

JUD. I said, *where*?

BILLY. Give over Jud, you're breaking me arm.

JUD. Where then?

BILLY. Monastery Farm.

> JUD *gets up and cuffs* BILLY *on the head.*

BILLY. You big git, you nearly broke me arm then.

JUD. I'll have to see about going round there with a gun.

BILLY. I'll tell t' farmer.

JUD. What's he got to do with it?

BILLY. He protects 'em.

JUD. Protects 'em, don't talk wet. Hawks are a menace to farmers. They eat all their poultry and everything.

BILLY. They dive down on their cows and carry 'em away an' all.

JUD. Funny bugger.

BILLY. Well you talk daft. Kestrels are only small. Kestrels only eat mice and insects and little birds sometimes. You should have seen 'em today, Jud. They go like lightning. I was laid watching one for hours this afternoon. They're t' best thing I've ever seen. She was sat on this telegraph post.

> JUD *looks in the mirror to knot his tie.*

JUD. I'm hoping I'll be laid watching a bird tonight but she'll not have feathers on, though.

BILLY. I was right underneath her.

JUD. Not all over, anyway.

BILLY. You ought to have seen 'em hovering though, Jud.

JUD. A few pints first.

BILLY. You ought to have seen 'em hovering then diving down.

JUD. Then straight across to t' Lyceum.

BILLY. Diving straight down behind this wall. Whoosh!

JUD. You think you know summat about 'em don't you?

BILLY. I know more about 'em than you anyroad.

JUD. You ought to an' all. You nearly live round in them woods. It's a wonder you don't turn into a wild-man.

JUD scratches his armpits and runs round the room imitating an ape.

Billy Casper, wild-man of t' woods. I ought to keep you in a cage, I'd make a bloody fortune.

JUD starts to throw BILLY around and BILLY's school exercise book up in the air again.

BILLY. Give over, Jud. Stop mucking about. Stop it. Stop it!

JUD. Up we go! Up! Up!! (*Reading cynically and laughing, hitting BILLY for the fun of it. BILLY trying throughout to get his exercise book back.*) 'I woke up and my mother says to me. Here, Billy, here's your breakfast in bed. There is bacon and egg and bread and butter and a big pot of tea. When I'd had my breakfast the sun was shining outside. I got dressed and go downstairs. Me and Dad and Mum live in a big house up on Moor Edge.' Cracked. Billy Casper, cracked wild-man of the woods.

JUD laughs cruelly. BILLY shouts. JUD returns to the ape imitation, pulling BILLY about. MRS CASPER enters.

MRS CASPER. You're a couple of noisy buggers, you two. What you been making him cry for, Jud?

JUD. I never touched him.

BILLY. Not much. Nearly broke me arm that's all.

JUD. I'll break your neck next time.

MRS CASPER. Shut it, both of you.

JUD. Well he's nowt but a big baby.

BILLY. And you're nowt but a big bully.

MRS CASPER. I said shut it. Jud, how did your horses gone on, Jud?

JUD. Not bad. I'd a double up.

MRS CASPER. You haven't have yer?

JUD. Aye.

MRS CASPER. How much?

JUD. Enough.

MRS CASPER. You might be treating me tonight then?

JUD. There's somebody treats you every night.

MRS CASPER. Oh, you shut it. (*Reflecting.*) It'd be nice. (*At sofa.*) Shift, Billy.

MRS CASPER. Where are you going tonight then, Jud, anywhere special?

JUD. Usual I suppose.

MRS CASPER. Well don't be coming home blind drunk again.

She pulls a pair of stockings from under the cushion, sniffs them, holds them up to the light to inspect them for ladders, and then puts them on.

JUD. You want to talk about coming home drunk.

MRS CASPER. I never come home drunk.

JUD. Not much you don't.

MRS CASPER. Well at least I'm not sick all over the house every Saturday night.

JUD. Not this house perhaps.

MRS CASPER. And what's that supposed to mean?

JUD. Well you don't come here every Saturday night, do you?

MRS CASPER. Don't be so cheeky. You're kidding. If I entertained as much as you I'll do all right wouldn't I? My God, the lasses you've been going out with lately.

JUD. Better than that idiot you bring home, in't it?

MRS CASPER. What idiot? D' you mean, Reg?

JUD. Aye. Are you gonna settle down with him then?

MRS CASPER. I don't know. Depends what you're looking for don't it?

JUD. Get home. Bath, changed and out. Not a care in t' world. What's more than that to look for?

MRS CASPER *is silent.* JUD *realises something's up.*

You don't want him? Reg? Nah. He's as tight as a camel's arse in a sandstorm.

MRS CASPER. You watch it.

JUD. Don't go marrying him. He's so tight-fisted he'd have his confetti on elastic.

MRS CASPER. Keep yer hand over yer mouth talking about him, 'cos I'm telling you it'll get you into trouble. You're not too big to have a good hiding, you.

JUD. He can't give it to me.

MRS CASPER. Who can't?

JUD. Idiot Reg.

MRS CASPER. You might find that he's bigger than what you think.

JUD. You what? He's got more chance of being struck by lightning than beating me.

MRS CASPER. Now shut it. It's every Saturday night the same. I get ready to go out and you upset me. You don't own this house, Jud.

JUD. No, but I will one day though, won't I?

MRS CASPER. Over my dead body.

JUD. That's what I say. I'll own it one day, won't I?

MRS CASPER. I'm sick of it, Jud. I go out to work every day of the week and the one day I go out for a drink you're at me. I'm that fed up I won't go.

JUD. Don't go then.

MRS CASPER. I won't.

JUD *has won.*

MRS CASPER. Have you had any tea, Billy?

BILLY. No.

MRS CASPER. Well get some then, you know where pantry is.

JUD *is putting on his shoes.* MRS CASPER *is at the other end of the sofa looking for her shoes.*

Shift, Billy.

JUD (*combing his hair in the mirror*). Hey, who's the smart looking kid in t' mirror? Some bird's going to be lucky tonight.

JUD *slips his jacket on.*

MRS CASPER. God's gift to woman. Fancy buying me a drink tonight then, Jud? Out of your winnings?

JUD (*ignoring her*). I hope it keeps fine for you.

JUD *walks out whistling.*

MRS CASPER. Seen me shoes, Billy love?

MRS CASPER *licks her fingers and tries to erase the scuff marks from her shoes, then steps into them.*

MRS CASPER. These could have done with a polish. Still never mind. It'll soon be dark. Billy, there's no ladders in these stockings is there?

BILLY (*submerged in his book, without looking up*). I can't see any.

MRS CASPER. That's summat, any road. What you doing with yourself tonight, love?

BILLY. Read me book.

MRS CASPER. That's nice. What's it about?

BILLY. Falconry. *A Falconer's Handbook* I'm going to get a young kestrel and train it.

MRS CASPER. A kestrel, what's that?

BILLY. A kestrel hawk, what do you think it is?

MRS CASPER. I say, what time is it?

BILLY. I've cleaned out shed, and I've built a little nesting box out of an orange box until –

MRS CASPER (*finding her watch and putting it on*). Ten to eight. I'm going to be late, as usual. Here, there's some money. Go and buy yourself some pop and some crisps or summat.

MRS CASPER *leaves.* BILLY *gets ready for bed and reads under the covers. Perhaps we hear the shipping forecast.*

BILLY (*reading*). Falconry is the art and sport of training birds of prey. Falconry is a sport because it is a type of hunting and it is often referred to as an art because some of the close relationships with the bird are based on the falconer's feelings and understanding of the hawk.

Beginning with a new bird manning the hawk must first be achieved. The falconer must train a bird to return to the gloved fist when called. When the falconer can get the hawk to perch on his fist, feed it morsels of food from his hand, and encourage the hawk to fly to the fist to take food he can train it to hunt birds, but will do so only with a lot of patience and time.

Scene 8

Flashback. Billy's Home. Night

JUD *returns home very drunk.* BILLY *pulls the covers round him and pretends to be asleep.* JUD *accidentally kicks the dustbins on his way inside.*

JUD. Shhh! Shhh! (*Calling.*) Billy. Billy.

BILLY *is still pretending to be asleep.* JUD *is swaying gently, as he climbs the stairs to the bedroom.*

Are you ashleep?

JUD *begins to get undressed and attempts to take off his trousers but loses his balance once his trousers are round his knees.*

Bleeding things.

JUD *nearly falls over.*

Whoa you bugger, whoa. Billy, wake up. Billy.

JUD *pulls at the bedclothes.*

Wake up, Billy, I said.

BILLY. Give over, Jud, I'm asleep.

JUD. Help me get these bleeding trousers off, Billy. I'm too
pisshed to get undreshed.

JUD *drops onto the bed giggling helplessly.*

Help me, Billy.

BILLY *gets out of bed and removes* JUD*'s trousers for him.
Once* JUD *is in bed:*

Turn light off, Billy, and get to bed.

BILLY. I'm fed up with this bloody game. Don't help will
you? It's every Saturday night alike.

JUD *snores loudly.*

Just like a pig snoring –a drunken pig – Jud, the drunken
pig. He stinks. You stink. Jud, the stinking drunken pig.

BILLY *shuts* JUD*'s mouth.*

JUD (*mumbling*). What's the matter? What's the matter?

BILLY. Go back to sleep you pig – hog –sow – you drunken
bastard. You don't like being called a bastard do you, you
bastard? You PIG?

BILLY *starts tapping* JUD *with one hand then the other
rhythmically, as he insults the slumped figure.*

Pig – hog – sow – drun – ken – bas – tard.

BILLY *repeats this and the slaps get louder.*

Pig – hog – sow – drun – ken – bas – tard.

BILLY *slowly moves around the bed.*

Bas-tard, Bas-tard, Drun-ken PIG.

Bas-tard, Bas-tard, Drun-ken PIG.

Faster and louder.

Pig Hog Sow, Drunken Bastard.

Pig Hog Sow, Drunken Bastard.

Bastard Bastard Drunken PIG.

Bastard Bastard Drunken –

BILLY *smacks* JUD *hard.* JUD *makes a loud noise and tries to sit up.* BILLY *grabs his shoes and runs out of the bedroom.*

JUD. Billy! Billy!

BILLY *is running through the city at night. He swings the lure. There is a huge full moon. Silence.* BILLY *hears an owl, imitates the sound and gets a reply. Gradually the* PUPILS *and* MR FARTHING *recreate the classroom, with their desks.* BILLY *climbs up, under and around them as before.*

We hear Kes in the distance. BILLY *reaches the monastery wall. He looks up at it, then carefully climbs up. The climb is not easy. He reaches the window, slaps the stone to disturb the parent kestrels. They fly out of the nest. He lifts one of the eyas kestrels out and examines it. He selects the one with the most feathers and places it carefully in the big pocket inside his jacket.*

BILLY. Did you hear 'em, Kes? Making mouth again. Gobby old cow. Drunken bastard. Do this, do that. I've to do everything in this house . . . well, they can shit. I'm fed up with being chased about. There's always somebody after me. And our Jud, he's the worst of the lot. He's always after me. Always has been. But, they won't catch me.

An Eagle for an Emperor, a Gryfalcon for a King; a Peregrine for a Prince, a Saker for a Knight, a Merlin for a Lady; a Goshawk for a Yeoman, a Sparrowhawk for a Priest, a Musket for a Holy-Water Clerk, a Kestrel for a Knave. A Kestrel for a Knave.

(*Triumphant.*) A Kestrel for a Knave.

Interval.

ACT TWO

Scene 9

After the Football Match, 12.25 pm

BOYS *are all talking amongst themselves, getting changed out of their football gear and into their uniforms, coming back from the showers, drying themselves off.*

ALLEN (*jumping to keep warm*). I hate games with him. It's always football. This weather and all. Me feet were frost-bitten out there. We haven't been in the gym for years now. Other classes do basketball sometimes. He just shouts 'On the field. On the field.' And he's like a chuffing carthorse.

MARTIN (*whistles*). Hey, he's coming.

MR SUGDEN *enters.*

MR SUGDEN. Stop bouncing, lad.

ALLEN. I'm still frozen, sir. I'm just jumping to keep warm, sir.

MR SUGDEN. Well stop jumping before I make you red hot. You should have done more running on the field. On the field, boy.

TIBBUT. Who were you playing as today, sir, Liverpool?

MR SUGDEN. Rubbish, lad. Do you mean to tell me that for ninety minutes you thought I was Liverpool. It was Manchester United against Spurs in the vital fifth round F.A. cup tie at Old Trafford.

TIBBUT. But Liverpool are red, aren't they sir?

MR SUGDEN. Yes, but they're all red. Shirts, shorts and stockings. These are Manchester United colours.

TIBBUT. Course they are, sir, I forgot. What position were you playing?

MR SUGDEN *turns round revealing a number ten on his back.*

TIBBUT. Bobby Charlton? I thought you were usually Dennis Law when you were Manchester United, sir?

MR SUGDEN. It was too cold to play as a striker today. I was scheming this morning. All over the field. Just like Charlton used to do.

TIBBUT. Law played all over t' field, sir. He wasn't just a striker.

MR SUGDEN. He didn't link like Charlton.

TIBBUT. Better player though, sir.

MR SUGDEN. Are you trying to tell me about football, Tibbut?

TIBBUT. No, sir.

MR SUGDEN. Well, shut up then, unless you'd rather do some maths for the rest of the term. Anyway, Dennis Law's in the wash this week.

TIBBUT. Well, United 2 Spurs 3, bad luck, sir.

MR SUGDEN. Shut it, Tibbut! Maths! Ten press-ups.

TIBBUT. Ah, sir, I can't do press-ups, I'm knackered.

MR SUGDEN. You'll be more than knackered in a minute. Press-ups, Now. One, two, three, four, five . . .

MR SUGDEN *moves down the line of* BOYS. *To* BILLY *who has nearly finished changing.*

Now, Casper, what happened out there? What were you doing, lad? What position do you play?

BILLY. Don't know, sir – I've not decided yet.

MR SUGDEN. Goal, Casper. You were in goal. You were in goal because you're no good elsewhere.

BILLY. It's not my fault we lost, sir. I told you I were no good in goal.

MR SUGDEN. Well it was your chance to learn wasn't it, Casper?

BILLY. I'm fed up of going in goal. I go in every week.

MR SUGDEN. You weren't just in goal, Casper. You were all over the goal. What are you Casper, an ape?

BILLY. You shouldn't blame me when I let 'em all through.

MR SUGDEN. Of course I blame you lad! You let three goals in, boy. You're too daft to laugh at, Casper. I'd like to drop you, Casper.

BILLY. Sir? Drop me from t' team, sir?

MR SUGDEN. No, Casper. Throw you up and drop you from a great bloody height.

Pause. BILLY *tries to give* MR SUGDEN *the borrowed football kit back.*

What's this?

BILLY. It's your shorts back, sir.

MR SUGDEN (*snatching them from him*). Shorts. I'm sick of you, Casper! I'll give you shorts, lad. Why is it every lesson the same old story? 'Please sir, I've got no kit.' Every lesson for four years! Next week no excuses, Casper. Why is it that everyone else can get some, but you can't?

BILLY. I don't know, sir. Me Mum says she won't buy me any. She says it's a waste of money. Especially now that I'm leaving.

MR SUGDEN. You haven't been leaving for four years, Casper! Anyway, you could have bought some out of your spending-money couldn't you?

BILLY. I don't like football, sir.

MR SUGDEN. What's that got to do with it?

BILLY. I don't know, sir. Anyway I don't get enough.

MR SUGDEN. Get a job then.

BILLY. I've got one, sir.

MR SUGDEN. Well then, you get paid don't you?

BILLY. Yes, sir, but I've got to give it to me Mum. I'm still paying her for me fines.

MR SUGDEN *bounces the ball on* BILLY*'s head.*

MR SUGDEN. Well you should keep out of trouble, lad.

BILLY. I've not been in trouble, sir, not for . . .

MR SUGDEN. Shut up, lad! Shut up, before you drive me crackers.

BILLY *starts to leave.*

In a hurry, Casper?

BILLY. Yes, sir, I've got to get home, sir.

MR SUGDEN. Why, Casper?

BILLY. To see me bird, sir.

MR SUGDEN. Does your father know you've got a girl-friend, Casper?

MACDOWALL. It's his kestrel, sir.

BILLY. It's better than you any day, MacDowall.

MR SUGDEN. Kestrel, Casper?

BILLY. Yes, sir.

MR SUGDEN. That must be stimulating, Casper.

BILLY. What's that, sir?

MR SUGDEN. Stimulating. S.T.I.M.I.L.A.T.I.N., stimulating.

BILLY. Can I get home, sir? For me dinner.

MR SUGDEN. What about the showers?

BILLY. I've had one, sir.

MR SUGDEN *gives him a back-hander knocking him across the room.*

BILLY. I have, sir. I was first through. Ask anybody, sir.

MR SUGDEN. I'll do just that. Have you seen Casper have a shower?

BOY 1. No, sir.

MR SUGDEN. Have you?

BOY 2. No, sir.

MR SUGDEN. What about you? Did Casper have a shower?

Two BOYS *shake their heads. Pause.*

Nobody seems to have seen you have a shower, Casper.

BILLY. Anyway me Mum says I haven't to have a shower, sir,
I've got a cold.

MR SUGDEN. Let's see your note then.

MR SUGDEN *holds out his hand.*

BILLY. Can I bring one this afternoon, sir?

MR SUGDEN. That's no good lad. I want one now. Any boy
wishing to be excused Physical Education or showers must
at the time of the lesson produce a sealed letter of
explanation signed by one of his parents or legal guardian.

BILLY. Oh go on, sir, I've to get home.

MR SUGDEN. You can get home, Casper, as soon as you've
had a shower.

BILLY. I've no towel, sir.

MR SUGDEN. Borrow one.

BILLY. Nobody'll lend me one.

MR SUGDEN (*amused*). Well you'll have to drip dry then,
won't you?

Nobody else laughs. BILLY *gets undressed quickly, and
runs into the showers. A wall is made by the* BOYS. BILLY
avoids the water as much as possible. He tries to leave.

MR SUGDEN. In a hurry, Casper? What's the rush, lad?

BILLY. Can I go now, sir?

The school bell rings.

MR SUGDEN. Go? You're two weeks late already.

MR SUGDEN *stations two* BOYS *by the shower entrance.*

Stay there and don't let him out.

BILLY *scours the mud off his arms and legs.* MR SUGDEN
swings the heater control to cold. BILLY *yells and tries to
get out past the boys stationed by the shower entrance.*

BILLY (*trying to escape*). Hey up, shift. Let me out you rotten dogs!

MR SUGDEN. Got a sweat on, Casper?

BILLY. Let me out, sir. Let me out.

MR SUGDEN. I thought you'd like a cooler after your exertions in goal.

BILLY. I'm frozen.

MR SUGDEN. Really?

BOY 1. Shall we let him out now, sir?

BOY 2. He'll get pneumonia, sir.

MR SUGDEN. I don't care what he gets.

BILLY. Give over, sir. It's not right, sir.

MR SUGDEN (*becoming increasingly frightening*). And was it right when you let that last goal in?

BILLY. I couldn't help it.

MR SUGDEN. Rubbish, lad. It's not a time for shirking. It may be called Games but there's more to it that playing. It's not the taking part it's the winning. You should be changed. Changed and out. On the field, boy. On the field! Games is no time for shirking. If you think I'm running my blood to water for ninety minutes and then having the game deliberately thrown away you've got another think coming. You're not going anywhere until you've had a proper wash.

Scene 10

The Playground, 12.40 pm

The playground has filled up with PUPILS. *Some smoking, others keeping watch, others playing ball. This extended until* BILLY *is dressed.*

MACDOWALL. Got owt, Casper?

BILLY *walks away.*

MACDOWALL. No. You never has. You just cadge all t' time. 'Casper the Cadger' that's what we should call you.

BILLY. I wouldn't give you owt if I had it, MacDowall.

MACDOWALL. I'll give you something in a minute. What's you going over there for, Casper?

BILLY. Mind your own business.

MACDOWALL. What's up? Don't you like company? They say your mother does! Takes after his mother. She's always running. After blokes, I've heard.

BILLY. Shut your mouth. Shut it, can't you!

MACDOWALL. Come and make me.

BILLY. You wouldn't say that to our Jud.

MACDOWALL. I bet I know someone who could do him.

BILLY. Who? Your Dad?

MACDOWALL. At least I've got a Dad. Yours ran off, me mam says. When your Dad caught your mam with your Uncle Mick.

BILLY. Shut it.

MACDOWALL. I've heard you've got more uncles than any kid in this City.

BILLY. Shut it, I said.

MACDOWALL. Is your Dad gonna run back and stick up for you?

BILLY. Shut it. Jud'll murder you.

MACDOWALL. Would he heck, he's nowt, your Jud.

BILLY. You what? He's cock of the Estate that's all.

MACDOWALL. Who says?

PUPILS (*gathering around. Under dialogue, very gradually, starting quietly*). Fight. Fight. Fight.

MACDOWALL. Your Jud won't stick up for you. He isn't even your brother.

BILLY. What is he then, me sister?

MACDOWALL. He's not your real brother, me mam says. They don't even call him Casper for a start.

BILLY. Course he's me brother! We live in t' same house don't we?

MACDOWALL. He don't even look like you. He's twice as big for a start. You're nowt like brothers.

MACDOWALL and BILLY fight. Firstly MACDOWALL pushes BILLY off with his foot, and as BILLY comes back he punches him hard which sends him flying.

MACDOWALL. Get away, you little squirt, before I spit on you and drown yer.

They continue to fight. A crowd of PUPILS surrounds them until MR FARTHING appears, blows his whistle and pushes his way through.

MR FARTHING. What's going on?

BILLY (*tearful*). It was him, sir! He started it.

MACDOWALL. I didn't, sir! It was him.

MR FARTHING. Shut up, both of you. It's the same old tale. It's nobody's fault and nobody started it. You just happened to be fighting for no reason at all. Don't look so sorry for yourself, Casper, you're not dead yet.

MACDOWALL. He will be when I get hold of him.

MR FARTHING. You're a brave lad aren't you MacDowall? He's just about your size, Casper, isn't he? Well if you're so keen on fighting why don't you pick on someone your own size eh? Eh?

MR FARTHING jabs MACDOWALL in the shoulder, and as MACDOWALL backs away, he walks after him, punctuating his speech with jabs.

What would you say if I pinned you to the floor and smacked you across the face? You'd say I was a bully, wouldn't you lad? And you'd be right because I'm bigger and stronger and I know I could beat you to a pulp before we started. Just like you know MacDowall with every boy you pick on.

MACDOWALL (*weakening*). I'll fetch me Dad.

MR FARTHING. Of course you will lad. And then do you
know what I'll do, MacDowall? I'll fetch mine. And do you
know, MacDowall that my Dad's the heavyweight champion
of the world? So what's going to happen to your Dad then,
eh? And what's going to happen to you?

He addresses the assembled PUPILS *who have been
enjoying the spectacle.*

I'm giving you lot ten seconds to get out of my sight. If I
see any face after that time, especially yours MacDowall,
I'll give its owner the biggest belting they've ever received.
One. Two. Three. Four. Five. Six. Seven . . .

They are gone. MR FARTHING *and* BILLY *remain.*

MR FARTHING. You always seem to cop it, don't you
Casper? Why is that?

BILLY. 'Cos everybody picks on me, that's why.

MR FARTHING. Perhaps that's because you're bad?

BILLY. I'm no worse than stacks of kids, but they just seem to
get away with it.

MR FARTHING. Have you been in trouble with the police
lately?

BILLY. No, sir.

MR FARTHING. Because you've reformed? Or because you
haven't been caught?

BILLY. I've reformed, sir. It's right, sir. I haven't done nowt
for ages now. That's why MacDowall's always picking on
me 'cos I don't knock about with their gang any more. But
since I stopped going out with 'em I stopped getting into
trouble.

MR FARTHING. What happened, did you have an argument or
something?

BILLY. No, sir, it was when I got my hawk. I got that
interested in it that it seemed to use all my time. It was
summer, you see, and I used to take it down our field at

nights. Then when dark nights came, I never got back in with 'em. Now I try to get hold of falconry books an' read up about 'em. I make new jesses and things, and sometimes I go down to t' shed and just sit with her. It's all right in there. We just sit there. It's stacks better than roaming t' street doing nowt. Cos that's all we used to do. Just roam about t' estate mucking about, fed up and frozen. We used to break into places and nick things just for bit of excitement. It was summat to do, that's all.

MR FARTHING. What about youth clubs? There's one open here three nights a week.

BILLY. I don't like youth clubs. I don't like games. We used to go into t' city, to t' pictures, or to a coffee bar sometimes. Cinema's closed down now and I don't have money for coffee bars. Anyroad, they can please 'emselves what they do. I'm not bothered now.

MR FARTHING. You're a lone wolf now, then?

BILLY. I'd like to be if only people'd leave me alone. There's always somebody after me though. Like this break. Like in class. They're always saying I'm a pest or a nuisance, they talk as though I like getting into trouble; but I don't, sir. And at home, if owt goes wrong on estate, police always come to our house. I feel like going out and doing summat just to spite 'em sometimes.

MR FARTHING. Just unlucky then?

BILLY. I don't know, sir. I seem to get into bother for nowt. You know, for daft things. This morning in t' hall, I wasn't doin' owt, I just dozed off that's all. I'd been up since before six, then I'd had to run round with t' papers then run home to have a look at t' hawk, then run to school. Well, I mean, you'd be tired, wouldn't you, sir?

MR FARTHING. I'd be exhausted.

BILLY. That's nowt to get t' stick for, is it, sir, being tired? You can't tell Gryce that. Do you know, sir, there was a lad this morning stood outside his room with us, he'd only brought a message from another teacher, and Mr Gryce gave him t' stick. (FARTHING *laughs*.) It's nowt to laugh at, sir. What about that kid? He was sick as a dog after. And this morning in English, it wasn't that I wasn't bothered, it was me hands, they were killing me! You can't concentrate when your hands are stinging like mad.

MR FARTHING. No, I don't suppose you can.

BILLY. It's always like that. Teachers are not bothered with us and we're not bothered with 'em.

MR FARTHING. Never mind, lad. You'll be leaving school in a few weeks, starting your first job, meeting new people. That's something to look forward to isn't it? (BILLY *doesn't respond*.) Have you got a job lined up yet?

BILLY. No, sir. I've got an interview this afternoon with Youth Employment.

MR FARTHING. What kind of job are you after?

BILLY. I'm not bothered, owt'll do me.

MR FARTHING. You'll try to get something that interests you though?

BILLY. I shan't have much choice shall I? I shall have to take what they've got.

MR FARTHING. I thought you'd been looking forward to leaving.

BILLY. I'm not bothered.

MR FARTHING. I thought you didn't like school.

BILLY. I don't, but that don't mean I'll like work does it? Still I'll get paid for not liking it, that's one thing.

MR FARTHING. Yes. Yes, I suppose it is.

BILLY. I might be able to save up and buy a goshawk then. I've been reading about 'em.

MR FARTHING. This hawk of yours, I'd like to see it sometime.

BILLY. Yes, sir.

MR FARTHING. When do you fly it?

BILLY. Dinner times. Shit. Sorry, sir, I gotta go.

MR FARTHING. Do you fly it at home?

BILLY. Yes, sir. In t' fields at t' back of our house.

MR FARTHING. That's Woods Avenue isn't it?

BILLY. Yes, sir. One hundred and twenty-four.

MR FARTHING. Right then, may I come down later?

BILLY (*unsure*). Yes, sir.

MR FARTHING. Good. Thanks, Billy.

    BILLY *runs off to . . .*

Scene 11

The Betting Shop, 2.00 pm

MRS ROSE *is here and a lot of* PUNTERS *reading newspapers, writing betting slips, smoking and listening to the racing commentary on the radio.*

BILLY. I say, mister, what odds are these two?

MAN. What you got?

BILLY. A Double: 'Crackpot' and 'Tell Him He's Dead'.

MAN (*he takes the betting slip*). 'Crackpot' . . . 100 to 6, and 'Tell Him He's Dead', that's . . . where is it? I've just been looking at that myself. 'Tell Him He's Dead', here it is: 4 to 1, second favourite.

    Gives the slip back to BILLY.

    100 to 6 and 4 to 1.

    Pause. BILLY *looks down at the slip.*

BILLY. Have they got a chance?

MAN. Now then, lad, how should I know?

BILLY. Would you back 'em?

    The MAN *consults the newspaper again.*

MAN. 'Tell Him He's Dead' has got a good chance. It's top weight. It's t' best horse in t' race. It must be or it wouldn't be top weight would it? I don't fancy t' other though. No form. Not even a jockey on it in here. It'll have some lad on it you can bet. No, I wouldn't bother with that one.

BILLY. You don't think they'll win then?

MAN. How've you got 'em – doubled?

BILLY. They're not mine, they're our Jud's.

MAN. He'll be all right if they do.

BILLY *moves to one side to consider a risk of his own.*

BILLY. Heads I place the bet. Tails I don't.

Tosses coin.

Heads. Shit. Best out of three.

BILLY *tosses the coin again.*

Tails.

BILLY *grins and walks round a little thinking what to do next.*

MAN. I can't see 'em winning myself though.

BILLY *smiles broadly and rushes out with the money.*

BILLY. Thanks, mister.

Scene 12

The field behind Billy's House, 2.30 pm

BILLY *is busy with the lure and Kes.*

MR FARTHING (*entering*). Casper.

BILLY. Bloody-Hell-fire.

BILLY *winds up the lure. They both address the bird from a distance.*

MR FARTHING. You think a lot about that kestrel, don't you, Billy?

BILLY. 'Course I do. Wouldn't you if she was yours? Me and me Dad reared a young fox-cub one time. Then let it go. It

were a little blinder. And magpies, jackdaws. I had a young
jay once; that was murder though, they're right hard to feed,
and it nearly died. I wouldn't have one again, they're best
left to their mothers.

MR FARTHING (*addressing Kes*). How is she, Casper?

BILLY. Sometimes she's alright, but sometimes she goes mad,
screaming and bating as though she'd never seen me before.

MR FARTHING. Bating? What's that?

BILLY. Trying to fly off, in a panic like.

MR FARTHING. I thought you said you'd trained her. Isn't
she tame?

BILLY. Is she heck tame. She's manned that's all. She's fierce
and she's wild, and she's not bothered about owt, not even
about me. It's a kind of pride, a kind of independence. She
looks you in t' eye and says 'Who the Hell are you, anyway?'

MR FARTHING *and* BILLY *exchange looks.*

Do you know, sir, I feel as though she's doing me a favour,
just letting me be her friend.

MR FARTHING. That's you respecting her.

BILLY. The most exciting time was when I let her fly free for
t' first time. I'd been flying Kes on t' creance for about a
week, and she was coming to me owt up to thirty, forty
yards, and it says in t' books that when it's coming this far,
straight away, it's ready to fly loose. I daren't though, sir.
I kept saying to myself, I'll just use t' creance today to make
sure, then I'll fly her free tomorrow. But when tomorrow
came I did the same thing again. Tomorrow. Tomorrow.
I did this for about a week than I got right mad with myself
'cos I knew I'd have to do it some day. So on t' last night
I didn't feed her up, just to make sure that she'd be sharp
set next morning. I hardly went to sleep that night, I was
thinking about it that much.

I wake up and I think right, if she flies off, she flies off, and
it can't be helped. I go down to t' shed. She's dead keen an
all, walking about on her shelf behind t' bars, and screaming
out when she sees me coming. I take her out in t' field and

try her on creance first time, and she comes first time, an'
she comes like a rocket. I think, right this time.

I unclip creance, take swivel off an let her hop on to t' fence
post. There is nowt stopping her now. She just stands there
with her jesses on. She can take off and there is nowt I can
do about it. I am terrified. I think, she's forced to go, she's
forced to, she'll just fly off and that'll be it. But she doesn't.
She just sits there looking around while I back off into t'
field. I go right into t' middle, then hold my glove up and
shout her.

Come on Kes! Come on then!

Nowt happened at first. Then, just as I go walk back to her,
she comes. You ought to have seen her. Straight as a die,
about a yard off t' floor. And t' speed! She comes twice as
fast as when she had creance on, 'cos it used to drag in t'
grass and slow her down. She comes like lightning, head
dead still, and her wings never make a sound, then wham!
Straight up onto my glove, claws out grabbing for t' meat.
I am that pleased I don't know what to do with myself.
Well, that's it. I've done it. I'd trained her. I trained her.

Pause.

MR FARTHING. Well done, Billy.

BILLY. It was a smashing feeling. You can't believe that you'll
be able to do it

MR FARTHING. There's something weird about hawks when
they fly, isn't there?

BILLY. You what, sir? Hawks are t' best flyers there is.

MR FARTHING. No, I mean . . . well, when they fly there's
something about it makes you feel strange.

BILLY. You mean everything goes dead quiet?

MR FARTHING. That's it.

BILLY. Other folks have noticed that an' all. Me Dad used to
say it's the same with owls. He said that he'd seen 'em
catching mice in our yard at night, and when they swoop
down you feel like poking your ears to make 'em pop.

MR FARTHING. How are things at home these days?

BILLY. All right, sir. Same as usual, I suppose.

MR FARTHING. Your Dad's not at home is he?

BILLY. No, sir.

MR FARTHING. Do you remember much about him?

BILLY. He left when I was six. All I remember is him pulling me up on his shoulder, and throwing me up in the air and catching me. Up high. And being caught. Over and over. Throw. Catch. Up. Down. Never falling.

MR FARTHING. Your Dad would have loved her, wouldn't he?

BILLY. You what, sir?

MR FARTHING. Kes. Don't you think he would have been proud of you?

BILLY. Don't know, sir. Haven't thought much about it.

MR FARTHING. I think he would have been very proud, Billy.

BILLY. My Dad?

MR FARTHING. Yes. Very very proud.

Pause.

Good lord! Look at the time. We'd better be off. I'll give you a lift back to school if you like. I'm in the car.

BILLY *shakes his head.*

What's the matter, wouldn't it do your reputation any good to be seen travelling with a teacher?

BILLY. It's not that, sir . . . I've one or two things to do first.

MR FARTHING. Please yourself then. But you're going to have to look sharp, or you'll be late.

BILLY. I know. I'll not be long.

MR FARTHING. Right. Thanks for our chat, Billy.

Scene 13

School Corridor and Butchers, 2.55 pm

School bell and the pit hooter both sound. The following scenes are inter-cut and are taking place simultaneously. From here to BILLY*'s return home the tension should gradually be increased.*

MR BEAL *the butcher is cutting meat on the counter as* BILLY *enters eating chips bought with the money he should have used for the bet.*

BILLY. Hi, Mister. A quarter of beef, please.

> JUD *is in the school and has cornered two pupils in the corridor.*

JUD. Have you seen our Billy?

DELAMORE. Billy who?

JUD. Casper. Have you seen him?

DELAMORE. No, not lately.

> *Back to the butchers.*

MR BEAL. My, them smell good.

BILLY. Do you want one?

MR BEAL (*taking a few chips*). Lovely.

> *Corridor.*

JUD Do you know him?

GIBBS. 'Course I know him.

> *Butchers.*

MR BEAL. Got 'em from Mrs Hartley's have you?

BILLY. Yes.

MR BEAL. Makes good chips does Mrs Hartley. Quarter of beef you say?

BILLY. Yes.

Corridor.

JUD. Do you think you will see him?

GIBBS. Don't know, might do, might not. It depends.

JUD. If you do, tell him you've seen me.

DELAMORE. What do you want him for anyway?

JUD. He should have put a bet on for me today but he didn't. He kept t' money. Tell him he's dead!

JUD *remains onstage looking for* BILLY *until the end of the* YOUTH EMPLOYMENT OFFICER *scene.*

MR BEAL*'s knife suddenly chops the meat violently and noisily.*

MR BEAL You've still got that bird then?

BILLY. Yes.

MR BEAL. Is it an owl?

BILLY. Kestrel.

MR BEAL. Where did you get it from?

BILLY. Found it.

MR BEAL. Is it tame?

BILLY. It's trained. I've trained it.

MR BEAL. Isn't it fierce?

BILLY. It is.

MR BEAL. Doesn't it kill things and eat 'em?

BILLY. 'Course it does. It kills little kids on bikes.

BILLY *and* MR BEAL *laugh.*

MR BEAL (*wraps the meat up*). Here. You can have that.

BILLY. For nowt?

MR BEAL. They're only scraps. I don't imagine you get much pocket money.

BILLY. Thanks. Do you want another chip?

MR BEAL. No thanks.

BILLY. See ya, then.

MR BEAL. See ya, Billy.

BILLY (*to himself*). Yeah, kids on bikes. (*Referring to parcel of scraps.*) This is a piece of leg off a kid it caught yesterday. When it catches 'em it sits on their handlebars and rips 'em into pieces. Eyes first.

BILLY *eats chips and invents a Desperate Dan story.* BILLY *is Dan the conquering hero. The story is crammed with laughter and* BILLY *is very happy. Nothing can possibly stop him now. He has food for Kes. And Dan. And chips.*

Mmm dinner. But who's this?

S – C – R – E – E – E – C – H!!

This is a stick up.

SQUIRT. SNIGGER.

Oh, no, quick setting glue!

Bring back that pie, you dirty scheming twister.

STOMP. STOMP. STOMP.

Where's my cow pie?

Hooray, it's Billy and Uncle Dan!

HEAVE! RIP! CRASH!

Now for you, you pesky pie-pincher.

GULP!

Sorry you can't *stick* around.

WALLOP! WHOOSH!

Take T – H – A – A – A – T – T – T ! ! !

C – R – A – S – H ! ! !

Where did he end up?

. . . in t' middle of next week, Uncle Dan.

Scene 14

School Corridor, 3.00 pm

DELAMORE. Where have you been? Everyone's been looking for you.

BILLY. Who has?

DELAMORE. Gryce Pudding and everybody.

BILLY. What for? I haven't done owt.

DELAMORE. Youth Employment. You should have gone for your interview last lesson.

GIBBS. And your Jud was up here too.

BILLY. Why?

GIBBS. He wants you. He's in school somewhere.

BILLY. What for?

DELAMORE. He's been hanging around a bit now. He's just been here looking for you.

BILLY. What for though?

GIBBS. I don't know. Summat about a bet.

BILLY. Christ. How long ago?

DELAMORE. Couple of minutes. We were just coming out of French. He was waiting outside. He must have thought that you were in our class.

GIBBS. I reckon he's going to thump you one. I should watch out. He looked right mad.

BILLY. Did he say owt?

DELAMORE. He asked where you were and kept shouting 'Tell him he's dead!' What you hiding from him for?

BILLY. Have you seen him since?

MR GRYCE *enters behind* BILLY. *The others see him and leave immediately.* MR GRYCE *hits* BILLY *twice. For a brief second* BILLY *thinks it may be* JUD. *He recoils and relaxes at the same time.*

MR GRYCE (*shouting*). And where do you think you've been, lad?

BILLY. Nowhere, sir.

MR GRYCE. Nowhere? Don't talk ridiculous lad. Who do you think you are – The Invisible Man? Wasn't that your illustrious brother, Casper?

BILLY. Where, sir?

MR GRYCE. I wouldn't have thought he was the type to pay his old school a visit. Are you all right, lad? What's the matter with you? Do you feel sick?

BILLY. No, sir.

MR GRYCE. Where have you been then lad?

BILLY. I did feel sick, sir, so I went to t' toilet.

MR GRYCE. And where were you? Down it? I sent prefects to the toilets. They said you weren't there.

BILLY. I must have gone outside, sir, for a breath of fresh air.

MR GRYCE. I'll give you fresh air.

BILLY. I've just come back in, sir.

MR GRYCE. What's the matter then, Casper? What are you looking for?

BILLY. Nowt, sir. What time is it, sir?

MR GRYCE. Time! Never mind the time, lad. What about your interview? Youth Employment. I've had the whole school out looking for you.

BILLY. I'm just going, sir.

MR GRYCE. Well get off then! Casper, look at me! And God help anyone who employs you. Don't you care, lad?

BILLY. Yes, sir.

MR GRYCE. Well, you could have fooled me.

School bell. Segue to . . .

YOUTH EMPLOYMENT OFFICER. Next! Well come in lad, if you're coming. Sit down, Walker.

BILLY. I'm not Walker.

YOUTH EMPLOYMENT OFFICER. According to my list, it should be Gerald Walker next. Ridley, Rye, Stenton and finally Walker.

BILLY. I'm Casper.

YOUTH EMPLOYMENT OFFICER. Oh yes. I should have seen you earlier, shouldn't I? Right. Now then, Casper, what kind of job have you in mind? (*Pause*) Well?

BILLY. Don't know, sir, haven't thought about it.

YOUTH EMPLOYMENT OFFICER. Well you're going to have to think about it. Have you looked around for anything yet?

BILLY. No, not yet.

YOUTH EMPLOYMENT OFFICER. Right then. Would you like to work in an office? Or would you prefer manual work?

BILLY. What's that, manual work?

YOUTH EMPLOYMENT OFFICER. It means working with your hands. For example building, farming, engineering, jobs like that, as opposed to pen-pushing jobs.

BILLY. I'd be all right working in an office, wouldn't I? I've a job to read and write.

YOUTH EMPLOYMENT OFFICER. Well, if it's manual work then, you could enter a trade as an apprentice? You know, as an electrician, or a bricklayer or something like that. Well, what do you think?

No reaction from BILLY.

Of course, the money isn't too good while you're serving your apprenticeship. You may find that lads of your own age who take dead-end jobs will be earning far more than you; but in those jobs there's no satisfaction or security, and if you do stick out at it you'll find it is worth your while. And whatever happens, at least you'll always have a trade at your fingertips won't you?

Well, what do you think about it? And as you've already said you feel better working with your hands, perhaps that would be your best bet. It would mean attending Technical College and studying for various examinations but nowadays most employers encourage their staff to take advantage of these facilities and allow them time off to attend – usually one day a week.

He gets up from his chair, looks out of the window, and continues talking.

On the other hand, if your firm wouldn't allow you time off during the day, and you were still keen to study, then you'd have to attend class in your own time. Some do it for years – two or three nights a week from leaving school until their mid twenties, when some take their Higher National Diplomas or even Degrees. But you've got to if you want to get on in life. And they'll all tell you that it's worth it in the end.

(*He turns round.*) Had you considered continuing your education in any form after leaving school?

No reaction from BILLY.

I say, are you listening to me?

BILLY. Yes.

YOUTH EMPLOYMENT OFFICER. You don't look as though you are. Now then, where were we? If nothing I've mentioned appeals to you, and if you can stand a hard day's graft and not mind getting dirty, then there are good opportunities in mining.

BILLY. I'm not going down t' pit.

YOUTH EMPLOYMENT OFFICER. Conditions have improved tremendously . . .

BILLY. I wouldn't be seen dead down t' pit.

YOUTH EMPLOYMENT OFFICER. Don't be put off by what you've heard.

BILLY. I wouldn't be seen dead down pit.

YOUTH EMPLOYMENT OFFICER. Well, what do you want to do then? There doesn't seem to be a job in England to suit you. What about hobbies? What hobbies have you got? What about gardening, keeping pigeons or constructing Meccano sets or anything like that?

BILLY *shakes his head.*

No hobbies at all?

BILLY (*standing*). Can I go now, sir?

YOUTH EMPLOYMENT OFFICER. What's the matter Casper? I haven't finished yet.

Takes a form and begins to fill it in.

Half the time you're like a cat on hot bricks – the other half you're not listening.

YOUTH EMPLOYMENT OFFICER *picks up a booklet.*

Here, take this form. It gives you all the relevant information concerned with leaving school and starting work. Things like sickness benefits, national insurance, pensions, salaries, etc. At the back there's a detachable form. When you want your cards fill it in and send it to the office. The address is given at the top. Have you got that?

BILLY *is not listening at all by this time and very anxious to get out of the room.*

Well take it then . . . and if you have any problem getting fixed up come in and see me. OK? Right, Casper, that's all.

BILLY *running. The following scene happens whilst the Betting Shop is established.*

Scene 15

The Field and Shed, 4.15 pm

BILLY. Kes! Kes!

Jud . . .

Jud! Mother!

Kes! Jud!

Kes! Kes! Come on then Kes!

Scene 16

The Betting Shop, 5.30 pm

MRS ROSE *from the betting shop enters sweeping or closing up the shop.* BILLY *runs to her.*

MRS ROSE. Oo! You dozy young devil. You scared me to death.

BILLY. Have you seen our Jud, missus?

MRS ROSE. I can see that you haven't or else you wouldn't be in one piece now.

BILLY. You have seen him then?

MRS ROSE. Seen him? He nearly ripped this place apart, that's all. He called me a welcher and all t' names under t' sun. He said I was trying to rob his eyes out. Then he threatened Tommy Leach with violence when he tried to put a word in, so Tommy walked out of t' shop. A right pantomime it was. I sent for Eric Clough and Eric Street in t' end to prove you never placed that bet.

BILLY. Has he been back?

MRS ROSE. They both won, you know. 'Crackpot' got a hundred to eight. 'Tell Him He's Dead' got four to one. He'd have had a tidy sum to draw.

BILLY. Do you know where he is now?

MRS ROSE. Why didn't you put that bet on?

BILLY. How do I know? I didn't know they were going to win, did I?

BILLY *leaves and starts to cry.*

MRS ROSE. You won't half get into trouble lad, when he gets hold of you.

BILLY *runs to . . .*

Scene 17

The Field, 7.00 pm

BILLY *is working the lure in the field, a handkerchief tied to the end if it. Calling to Kes all the time. He shortens the chord and swings it round so fast that it unravels. Then he lets it go and shoots it up in the air. He runs to it as it falls to the ground. This happens several times.*

BILLY. Kes! Kes! Come on then Kes!

Come on Kes! Come on then!

Kes! Kes! Kes!

Kes! Kes! Kes!

Kes! Kes! Kes!

BILLY *runs to . . .*

Scene 18

Billy's House, 8.00 pm

BILLY *bursts in through the kitchen and into the living room. The radio is playing.* JUD *is drinking tea.* MRS CASPER *is sitting at the table reading a magazine.*

BILLY. Where is it? What have you done with it?

MRS CASPER. Where've you been till now? Shut that door, Billy, there's a terrible draught behind you. Get some tea.

BILLY. I said where is it?

JUD *continues to read the comic, dipping biscuits into his tea, then suddenly:*

JUD (*shouts*). What're you staring at?

MRS CASPER. What's going off, what's all t' bloody shouting about?

BILLY. Ask him, he knows what it's all about.

JUD. Yes lad, and you'd have known if I'd got hold of you earlier.

MRS CASPER. Know what, what are you both talking about?

BILLY *is very distressed.*

Now what's the matter with you?

BILLY *can only point to* JUD.

What you done to him now, Jud?

JUD. It's his fault, if he'd put that bet on like he was told there'd have been none of this.

MRS CASPER. Didn't he? I told him before I went to work this morning.

JUD. Did he bloody hell.

MRS CASPER. I told you not to forget, Billy.

JUD. He didn't forget, he spent t' money.

MRS CASPER. And what happened, did they win?

JUD. Win! I'd have had a fair whack to draw if he'd kept his thieving hands to himself!

MRS CASPER. Oh, Billy, you've done it once too often this time.

JUD. They both won you know. A hundred to eight and four to one, they came in. I knew it an' all! 'Tell-Him-He's-Dead', was a cert, and I've been following that 'Crackpot' all season. It was forced to win sometime. I could have had a week off work with that money.

MRS CASPER. Well, what's he crying about then?

BILLY. Because he's killed me hawk instead, that's why.

MRS CASPER. You never have, have you, Jud?

BILLY. He has, I know he has, just because he couldn't catch me.

MRS CASPER. Have you, Jud?

JUD. All right then, so I've killed it. What are you going to do about it?

BILLY *screams an agonising cry and collapses onto the floor or sofa. He then rushes round to* MRS CASPER. *He tries to bury his face against her. She holds him off, embarrassed and pushes him to the floor.*

MRS CASPER. Give over then, Billy. Don't be so daft.

JUD. It was its own stupid fault! I was only going to let it go, but it wouldn't get out of its hut. And every time I tried to shift it, it kept lashing out at my hands with its claws. Look at them, they're scratched to ribbons!

BILLY. You bastard! You big rotten bastard.

JUD. Don't call me a bastard, else you'll be next to get it.

BILLY. You bastard! You fucking bastard!

MRS CASPER. Shut up, Billy, I'm not having that kind of language in here.

BILLY. Well do summat then! Do summat to him!

MRS CASPER. Where is it Jud? What have you done with it?

JUD. It's in the bin. Where it belongs.

BILLY runs out to the dustbin, feels inside and finds the dead hawk. BILLY returns to the living room, possibly with the dead bird. If it remains in the dustbin BILLY tries to get MRS CASPER to the bin, if there is a bird, BILLY waves it around the room.

BILLY. Have you seen what he's done, Mum?

MRS CASPER. It's a shame love, but it can't be helped.

BILLY. Come and look at it though. Look what he's done.

MRS CASPER. It was a rotten trick, Jud.

JUD. It was a rotten trick what he did, wan't it?

MRS CASPER. I know but you know how much he thought about that bird.

BILLY. It's not fair on him, Mum. It's not fair.

MRS CASPER. I know, but it's done now, so there's nowt we can do about it, is there?

BILLY. What about him though, what are you doin' to him?

MRS CASPER. What can I do?

BILLY. Hit him! Gi' him a good hiding! Gi' him some fist!

JUD. I'd like to see her.

MRS CASPER. Talk sense, Billy. How can I hit him?

BILLY. You never do owt to him, he gets away with everything.

MRS CASPER. Oh, shut up now. You've cried long enough about it.

BILLY. You're not bothered about owt, you.

MRS CASPER. 'Course I'm bothered, but it's only a bird. You can get another, can't you?

BILLY knocks the cup of tea out of her hand, clears the table and attacks JUD. *They fight for some time.* BILLY *scratching, leaping high on* JUD's *back.* JUD *puts* BILLY *on the ground, and is going to go for him but* BILLY *escapes.*

MRS CASPER (*through the fighting*). What are you doin'? Billy, stop it. Jud, leave him alone! Stop it, both of you!

She tries to come between them. BILLY *swings his fist at her, runs out of the house.*

Billy! Billy, come back here.

JUD. Billy, come back here you young bugger!

BILLY. You'll not catch me! You'll never catch me! Never, never!

BILLY *runs off to . . .*

Scene 19

The Cinema, 11.00 pm

It is raining. Distant traffic.

BILLY. Dad? Dad, are you here? It's raining outside so I broke in. Nobody knows I'm here.

BILLY *switches on a torch or lights a match.*

Bloody-Hell-fire it's cold. Smells of cats' piss.

BILLY *throws a stone. Windows smash, light from outside floods into the cinema. He reads.*

The Palace Picture House. Forthcoming Attractions. Nowt. The Big Picture. Billy as hero. Billy on t' screen. Big Billy. Kes on my arm. Big Kes. Close up. Technicolor. Imagine. It's starting. The Big Picture. Wait a minute, I've seen this one. Look, that's me Dad and me. Billy as hero. Billy on t' screen. Big Billy. Close up. Technicolor. No, you don't understand. That's my Dad and me.

I wake up and my mother says to me. Here, Billy, here's your breakfast in bed. There is bacon and egg and bread and butter and a big pot of tea. When I'd had my breakfast t' sun was shining outside. I get dressed and go downstairs. We live in a big house up on Moor Edge. There are carpets on t' floor, on t' stairs and in t' hall. And there is central heating. When I got downstairs I say, 'Where's our Jud?' 'He's going in t' army,' my mother says, 'and he's not coming back. But your Dad's coming back instead.' There is a big fire in t' room and my Dad comes in carrying his case that he took away with him. I hadn't seen him for a long time but he was just the same as when he went away. He throws me up in the air. So high. So very very high.

I was glad he had come back and that our Jud had gone away. When I go to school all t' teachers are good to me. They say 'Hello, Billy, how are you getting on?' and they all pat me on the head and smile. And we do interesting things all day. When I get home my mother said that she isn't going to work no more. We all have chips and beans for our tea. We get ready and come out to t' pictures.

Look, Dad! Billy casting Kes off, flying low, one rapid wide circuit, then leisurely gaining height, hovering and sliding sideways a few yards. Kes waiting while Billy walks forward. Perfectly clear. Hovering and gaining height. Higher. Higher. (*Suddenly sadder.*) The picture on the screen blurs. Dad? Blurs and fades. Dad blurs and fades.

Then we all go home and have fish and chips for our supper.

'Catch me, Dad. Catch me. Don't let me fall. Don't ever let me fall.'

The End.